BRISTOL INTRODUCTIONS

R. G. Collingwood
An Introduction

THOEMMES

R. G. COLLINGWOOD

An Introduction

Peter Johnson

Preface by
Ray Monk

Series Editor
University of Southampton

THOEMMES PRESS

Published in 1998 by

Thoemmes Press
11 Great George Street
Bristol BS1 5RR, England

US office: Distribution and Marketing
22883 Quicksilver Drive
Dulles, Virginia 20166, USA

ISBN 1 85506 530 4 – Hardback
ISBN 1 85506 531 2 – Paperback

British Library Cataloguing-in-Publication Data

A catalogue record of this title is available
from the British Library

To S. J.

CONTENTS

PREFACE

In the history of twentieth-century British philosophy, R. G. Collingwood cuts a lonely figure, swimming against every identifiable tide. During his time as Waynflete Professor of Metaphysics at Oxford, the two main currents of philosophical thought were the strident metaphysical realism of those now-forgotten figures, H. A. Prichard and H. W. B. Joseph, and the analytic philosophy introduced into Oxford from Cambridge by Gilbert Ryle and the young A. J. Ayer. Collingwood set his face resolutely against both. At a time when British philosophy lost interest in history, declared metaphysics to be 'nonsense', and banished aesthetics to the margins of the discipline, Collingwood practised a kind of philosophy that put history, metaphysics and aesthetics at the very centre of its concerns.

Now, however, with the analytic tradition in crisis and a growing feeling that philosophers ought, after all, to have something to say about the things that matter to people, the time may be right for a reassessment of Collingwood's work. Peter Johnson's elegantly written and sympathetic introduction is, therefore, extremely timely. Johnson presents his study as a contribution to a conversation between Collingwood and present-day philosophers, and he does a marvellous job at picking out from Collingwood's work arguments that address themselves to issues that are alive today. What is the relationship between thought and language? Can philosophy hope to aspire to the exact methods of the physical sciences? What role can or should formal logic play in philosophy? To what extent is our understanding of ourselves neccessarily historical? What *is* understanding? On all these questions Johnson finds telling similarities and contrasts between the views of Collingwood and those of the later Wittgenstein, who thus emerges as one of the chief participants in the conversation that Johnson initiates. In the process, one feels that if Collingwood had lived for a few more decades, he would have found himself a rather less isolated figure.

Wittgenstein once wrote: 'We feel that even if all possible scientific questions were answered, the problems of life would remain untouched.' In the same spirit, Collingwood insisted that science had little or nothing to say on the fundamental questions that concern the philosopher. This is not – *pace* the positive tradition – because those questions are nonsensical, but simply because they are not scientific questions and that, therefore, other methods must be used in addressing them. The method Collingwood adopted was what he called 'the logic of question and answer', Collingwood's claims for which Johnson subjects to gentle but penetrating criticism. Even if one does not accept all Collingwood's claims for this method, however, it is still possible to believe that in rejecting the scientism that informs the main current of philosophical opinion, he had hit an important nail on the head.

It is also possible to believe that Collingwood was on the right lines in drawing connections between the understanding we seek in philosophy and that which we seek in history and art. Perhaps he was also right to insist that, fundamentally, this consists in an attempt to understand ourselves. In any case, one of the very great merits of Johnson's fine book is that it enables us to see the interconnectedness of Collingwood's thinking on metaphysics, history and art, and to see also how his passionate commitment to liberal civility in politics was essentially linked to the single world-view that informed everything he wrote.

Grand metaphysical systems, especially those of an Idealist stamp, were unfashionable when Collingwood was writing and have remained so ever since. However, in the details of Collingwood's thinking, Johnson finds much that speaks to our present concerns. Philosophical writing, Collingwood wrote, is 'essentially a confession, a search by the mind for its own failings and an attempt to remedy them by recognizing them'. Now that many within the analytic tradition ('that numerous and frightful offspring of propositonal logic out of illiteracy', as Collingwood once described it) have recognized its failings, perhaps it is time we allowed Collingwood's voice a greater part in our philosophical conversations. Peter Johnson's book, by introducing him to the present company, inviting him to speak and stilling some of the shriller voices that hitherto have drowned him out, enables us all to hear what he has to say.

Ray Monk
University of Southampton, 1998

ACKNOWLEDGEMENTS

I would like to thank James Connelly for the many discussions I have had with him about Collingwood; Ray Monk for writing the Preface; Jane Williamson of Thoemmes Press for her patience; Mrs Jean Ballard for setting aside her own work in order to produce a typescript, often against the clock; my colleagues in the Philosophy Department who never quite tired of asking how the book was progressing; my wife, Sue, for casting her experienced and professional eye over the manuscript; and, finally, successive generations of writers on Collingwood who have influenced my own thinking.

ABBREVIATIONS

a) Works by Collingwood

A	*An Autobiography* (1939)
EM	*An Essay on Metaphysics* (1940)
EPH	*Essays in the Philosophy of History* (1965)
EPM	*An Essay on Philosophical Method* (1933)
EPP	*Essays in Political Philosophy* (1989)
IH	*The Idea of History* (1946 and 1993)
NL	*The New Leviathan* (1942 and 1992)
PA	*The Principles of Art* (1938)
RP	*Religion and Philosophy* (1916)
SRC	'Science, Religion and Civilization' (1930) (Collingwood MS, Burchnall, 1/7, p. 6)
SM	*Speculum Mentis* (1924)

b) Works by Others

AL	G. Berkeley, *Alciphron or the Minute Philosopher* (1950)
CP	G. Ryle, *Collected Papers* (1971)
EM	M. Oakeshott, *Experience and its Modes* (1933)
FF	B. Russell, *Fact and Fiction* (1961)
LWAM	N. Malcolm, *Ludwig Wittgenstein: A Memoir* (1962)
OC	L. Wittgenstein, *On Certainty* (1969)
PI	L. Wittgenstein, *Philosophical Investigations* (1953)
PTC	A. J. Ayer, *Philosophy in the Twentieth Century* (1982)
RK	C. Carrington, *Rudyard Kipling, His Life and Work* (1978)
TLP	L. Wittgenstein, *Tractatus Logico-Philosophicus* (1961)

INTRODUCTION

For some, R. G. Collingwood was a philosopher who came very close to genius. A polymath, he is, nevertheless, often thought to be marginal to the mainstream of twentieth-century philosophy. Fiercely critical of analytical philosophy though he was, Collingwood has been read as a representative of a brand of philosophical idealism best left firmly buried. He presents us, therefore, with something of a puzzle. Since philosophers are concerned with puzzles, questioning Collingwood's philosophy should prove instructive. That is what I intend to do in this book.

Collingwood is known to us as a philosopher who was also a distinguished historian. As a philosopher, Collingwood's reputation rests largely on his extensive writings about art, history and the nature of philosophy itself. As an historian, he wrote mainly on the archaeology of Roman Britain. As a philosopher, Collingwood argued that the crucial question for modern philosophy to answer was the nature of its relation to history. Much of what Collingwood says about this relation strikes us as innovative and topical. So when Collingwood explores philosophy historically and history philosophically he is raising issues which are central to the way many contemporary philosophers speak about the status of philosophy.

Collingwood's philosophical writings are known both to philosophers and non-philosophers. Unlike Russell, for example, who tended to write for, and be read by, either one of these camps or the other, Collingwood appeals to both. There is a good reason for this. Philosophy, in Collingwood's view, cannot progress if it cuts itself off from the experience it tries to understand. Thus, a philosophy of art depends on knowing what it is to be an artist, a philosophy of history on grasping the activity of an historian. Artists and historians read Collingwood in this light. They read him in the knowledge that his philosophical clarification of art and history contains a sure practical understanding of what they involve. But what of philosophers when they turn to Collingwood for enlightenment?

For philosophers it is not enough that Collingwood understands art as an artist or history as an historian: what he says about them as a philosopher must be true. For Collingwood, a philosophical account of human activities proceeds, in part, by attending closely to the concepts through which such activities understand themselves. So a philosophy of art aims to articulate what is distinctive about the language of art, a philosophy of history what is distinctive about the nature of historical vocabulary, and so on. But what *is* the language appropriate to art or to history, and how can this be determined by philosophy? Such questions imply that philosophy must be as much concerned with the character of its own procedures as it is with the practice of art or history. Philosophical attentiveness, therefore, is, in large measure, a matter of bringing the right philosophical methods to bear on the activity under investigation. In philosophy, Collingwood may be taken as saying, questions of truth and questions of method are never very far apart.

In this short book on Collingwood I aim to do two things: first, to give a clear outline of Collingwood's thought. The branches of his philosophy I examine include his discussions of language, logic and metaphysics where his ideas are often thought to be radical and not a little quirky, as well as his more establishment contributions in art, politics and the philosophy of history. Given Collingwood's stress on the importance of reaching a 'rapprochement' (his term – *A*, p. 147) between theory and practice I spend some time on his view of the relation between philosophy and life, even though his thinking in this area seems less rewarding. My second aim is to show where and why I agree or disagree with what he says.

Of course, disagreeing with Collingwood requires a knowledge of what he stands for, but philosophy would be an arid business if it confined itself solely to exegesis. Disagreeing with Collingwood seems to ask for a preparedness to approach him in terms that are not always his. It signifies a willingness to shed those ways of speaking which are often most characteristic of his style in philosophy. It concerns differences over Collingwood's account of method in philosophy as much as it does differences over its results. It embraces his understanding of the relation between philosophy and other human activities as well as his view of the nature of the latter, of what makes them differ from philosophy and from each other.

To engage Collingwood in argument is the quintessential philosophical response, but what does it require of us? Are we to treat Collingwood as our contemporary, criticizing his ideas in the way we would another philosopher in a seminar? The historical distance between us and Collingwood certainly makes him less remote than Socrates, Descartes or Hegel, but why should any distance make a difference to our understanding if the questions which concern one philosopher must concern them all? Disagreeing with Collingwood, however, is plainly not like disagreeing with a contemporary. The context of Collingwood's thought is substantially different from our own; philosophy has moved on, developing new techniques and asking different questions. We can, however, overstate this objection. Some philosophers do genuinely anticipate later theories. It is intolerably parochial to assume that our way of formulating philosophical problems is the only certain way. That some kinds of philosophical talk have become unfashionable does not mean that they are beyond restoration or translation into more relevant terms. Indeed, in Collingwood's own way of speaking, the present and the past do not stand as distinct entities to each other, sunk in permanent separation, but are better conceived as interrelated, the past living in and nourishing the present when the wit exists to identify and reconstruct it.

Treating Collingwood as our contemporary presents another problem. How do we know that the Collingwood we engage with is not made of straw, is merely a vehicle for *our* philosophical interests rather than his own? Collingwood speaks to us only through his texts, so the dialogue with him must remain one-sided unless we can extrapolate his response to criticism from the spirit of his philosophy, the methods we know he employed, or his way of dealing with similar difficulties.

There is a related problem here. To argue with Collingwood is to argue with his texts, but which texts? This is not as straightforward a question as it appears. In 1978 the bulk of Collingwood's manuscripts were deposited in the Bodleian Library, Oxford. Collingwood's thought is now not represented only by the published works, or, indeed, since a number of his manuscripts have been published, only by work that he himself authorized for publication. In giving priority to philosophical criticism of Collingwood I shall take a robustly pragmatic stance on this question. Where Collingwood's arguments seem to me to involve difficulties, a challenge will be laid down, irrespective of the source of the argument.

Discussing Collingwood's arguments individually on their merits would seem to be standard philosophical procedure, but it is not without its critics. Collingwood's thought, it is claimed, exhibits major inconsistencies. Within important areas such as the relation between philosophy and history, the status of metaphysics, and the nature of art, Collingwood's arguments are thought to be at variance with one another. Since we do not here know what Collingwood means to stand for, it is often thought necessary to search for a unity in his work. We should examine Collingwood's thought in the round. The individual arguments it contains become intelligible only against the background of the whole.

It is not surprising that on the basis of this analysis attention should have concentrated on the development of Collingwood's thought. Questions of interpretation now become paramount. Do Collingwood's later views reveal a radical conversion to historicism? Is metaphysics collapsed into history? Is Collingwood's philosophy divisible into periods – the early, middle and late Collingwood – and, if so, are the views he expressed at these different times compatible? We can listen to Collingwood only, it seems, if he speaks in one voice. But which voice would that be?

Attending to Collingwood as a spokesman for one of Ryle's famous 'Isms' – an Idealist, say, locked in battle with Realists and Materialists – would seem to prejudge his views and, in any case, would run up against Collingwood's own explicit disavowal of such titles. If we have to see Collingwood in the round then this is clearly the least satisfactory way of doing it. A more refined technique, but a horse from the same stable, is to attempt to show how Collingwood's thought evolved in the light of his intentions. Using Collingwood's own account of his intellectual development in *An Autobiography* as an essential guide it is possible on the basis of both published and unpublished material to reconstruct his thought as a coherent whole. Assiduous practitioners of this method have even detected a dialectical structure which shapes his writing, each distinct argument in it being a detailed working out at different analytical levels of the design of the whole.

This form of literary detective work certainly impinges on philosophy, but that it is not philosophy should be clear enough. Collingwood's arguments are intelligible in their own right. In taking Collingwood to be saying this rather than that about a specific topic, colours are firmly nailed, and it is up to anyone who disagrees to show why they should be hauled down.

When I stress the distinction between the development of Collingwood's thought and its place in our own I am not defending anything startling, apart from a stance not usually taken in studies of Collingwood. In our contemporary perspective, Collingwood's arguments are tested to discover whether or not they do actually further our grasp of a problem and how it can be solved. Collingwood's thinking about, say, the philosophy of history, has, of course, shaped our own in many different ways, but this is clearly a separate issue from the nature of his intellectual development.

Consider an example from Collingwood's political philosophy. In contemporary political philosophy there is considerable agreement that in any discussion of political decency justice has to be the main load-bearing concept. By what philosophical method can the principles of justice be derived? What form should such principles take and what political arrangements are consistent with them? These are the central questions. But Collingwood says nothing at all about justice.

This means that when we treat Collingwood as our contemporary we discover that he does not speak about justice as we do. Does this diminish his philosophical interest? The answer must be that it does not. The course taken by our conversation with him is not set in advance, since its value to us is significantly dependent on the kind of philosophical attention that *we* bring to it. So the absence in Collingwood of any discussion of justice may encourage us to rethink our assumptions regarding the importance of justice. Is justice truly a foundational political value or are there deeper moral considerations beyond justice? Likewise, since this is a conversation, we probe Collingwood's texts for arguments strong enough to explain why he gives justice such scant attention. Is his general account of moral reasoning sufficient to capture the nature of justice? Without a secure grasp of civility, say, is our sense of the importance of justice too easily diminished?

I have spoken of engagement with Collingwood as a conversation. When well-conducted, its merits will be those found in any conversation – a feeling of mutual exploration, frank exchange of views and a willingness to accept criticism which prompts the discussion along. Conversation understood in this way requires no validation external to itself. It posits no godlike vantage point from which its content or direction should be assessed. It takes no interest in the history of its participants' opinions, unless this happens to bear on their present concerns. While how Collingwood found his philosophical voice *is* a matter of unravelling the evolution of his thought, what that voice says now – the part it plays in conversation with us – is not a question of autobiographical or biographical fact, but argument.

Thus, treating Collingwood as a fellow conversationalist means considering his arguments as possible solutions to philosophical problems. It means treating alleged inconsistencies in his thought as possible inconsistencies in the solutions to those problems. Thus, the charge that Collingwood in his later thought collapsed philosophy into history is taken to refer not to the development of his thought, but to any possible collapse. Likewise, Collingwood's view that certain presuppositions are so fundamental to human life that truth/falsity criteria do not apply to them is taken to refer to a possible view. In political philosophy, the nature of Collingwood's liberalism – articulated without reference to justice – is taken as a possible articulation, and so on.

How Collingwood contributes to the conversation I am imagining is not, of course, entirely within his command. His voice has to be reconstructed and in this exercise there is scope for disagreement. Such latitude is not unlimited, however. Collingwood's thought contains a number of key theses on, for example, the nature of art, philosophy and the historical imagination, so that criticism can be directed with the reasonable certainty that it has a target to hit. Since the aim is to test Collingwood's arguments rather than explore the internal coherence of his thought I shall devote more houseroom to discussion rather than exposition of his views. Presenting these in summary form – in a brief, introductory, but not, I hope, unfair way – is likely to elicit contesting interpretations; if so, then they must show why my criticism is mistaken, shallow or inappropriate.

So as not to interrupt the flow in such a short book I have kept quotations from Collingwood and others to a minimum. References, too, are similarly confined to barracks. The secondary literature on Collingwood (see bibliography of Works by Others), especially to do with the development of his thought, is now so substantial that it is no longer possible to consider him a neglected figure, although the exact standing of his work in a contemporary philosophical context is less clear-cut. In this book I shall not appraise Collingwood or even attempt to 'situate' him in the history of modern philosophy. Rather my aim is the modest one of pursuing a conversation with him to discover what he has to say, and whether or not it clarifies or obscures the subjects which crop up for discussion. Since his voice in this conversation does not come from a void I shall spend a short time in the next chapter outlining his life and the main influences on it.

Chapter 1
A LIFE AND ITS INFLUENCES

On Collingwood's own account his first contact with philosophy occurred at the age of eight when he took down from his father's library shelves a copy of T. K. Abbott's translation of Kant's *Grundlegung Zur Metaphysik der Sitten* (A, p. 3). Like Russell, who, again on his own account, had a not dissimilar experience in relation to mathematics when he first read Newton's *Principia*, in 'a three-volume Latin edition of 1760' (*FF*, p. 42), Collingwood claimed to have felt exhilarated by the feeling that the book was telling him what his life's work would be. Collingwood's life did not turn out to be eventful on a grand scale as Russell's did; in both, however, family life shapes their later selves. Collingwood's adult cosmology reflects his first world. What he learnt in childhood and youth tells us a great deal about the character and direction of his later life.

R. G. Collingwood was born on 22 February 1889 at Gillhead, Cartmel Fell, in the Lake District. He was the third child of William Gershom Collingwood (1854–1932), a noted writer, archaeologist and antiquary, and Edith Mary Collingwood (1857–1928), an established painter and musician. Collingwood speaks (A, p. 3) of listening to his mother playing piano sonatas by Chopin and Beethoven before breakfast and sometimes in the evening. He was, up to the age of thirteen, educated at home where he was taught Latin and Greek by his father – his 'first and best' teacher, as he was later to describe him in the Dedication to *Speculum Mentis*. In this environment of encouragement and hard but enjoyable work the young Collingwood absorbed the ideals which guided Collingwood family life. Talking of this period in his autobiography (*A*, p. 4), Collingwood describes the sensation he experienced as a child of wanting to think, but not knowing what he should think about.

How Collingwood found subjects to think about is in large measure the story of the thought of others and how they helped to determine his cast of mind. Here the crucial, early influence is, of course, the example set by Collingwood's parents. Both were practising artists – their artistic life being, in fact, a part of their inheritance since W. G. Collingwood's father was William Collingwood (1819–1903), a well-known English water-colourist. R. G. Collingwood and his sisters shared fully in this way of life, making sketches of each other, paying close attention to their parents' methods of painting, imitating them and being taught how to improve their own skills in precise drawing and ornament. From the many hours spent in these activities Collingwood learned the importance of a sure grasp of the practical nature of the artist's life. He came to appreciate that knowledge in art is knowledge in use, that artistic speculation comes second place to the scrape of the brush or crayon.

Habits of precise observation and expression were acquired, too, in the time Collingwood spent accompanying his father, an eminent historian of Roman Britain (especially of Northumbria and the Lake District), on archaeological investigation. The experience of working closely with him in examining artefacts and making drawings of locations and sculptures formed in Collingwood the routines of systematic enquiry and clear formulation of questions which characterize his later writing. Collingwood's mature philosophy of art and his philosophy of history both owe a great deal to his view that it is necessary for a philosopher to understand these activities from within, and it is difficult to believe that the origins of this philosophical trait are not to be found in the impact of his early education.

Collingwood's upbringing encouraged habits of precise thought and clear enquiry, but it also embodied a substantial picture of how life should be lived. The way of life absorbed by the young Collingwood was one animated by ideals. A fulfilled human life is one that gives deepest expression to the many sidedness of human nature. Art, science, history, religion and philosophy satisfy distinct spiritual needs; each contributes in its own way to our sense of being complete. This fundamental commitment to the unity of thought and action is implicit in the way Collingwood's cast of mind was formed. It owes much to the general influence of Ruskin on the Collingwood family ethos (W. G. Collingwood was Ruskin's friend, biographer and last secretary), but it is found, too, in the Evangelicalism of William Collingwood, especially in his belief in the inseparability of truth and beauty.

How Collingwood found a voice of his own owed much to the influence of his early years. Little was added to this process of self-discovery by the time he spent at Rugby, but after 1908, when he went up to University College, Oxford, it gathered momentum and increased its range to include the subjects that were to preoccupy him for the rest of his philosophical life. Gilbert Ryle remarks that to get to grips with a philosopher we need to discover not only his 'intellectual worries', but his 'overriding worry' (*CP*, I, p. ix). In Collingwood's case, this 'big' worry is not difficult to discern. We have seen how Collingwood's formative years were shaped by his family's way of life. The ideals which gave this life its distinctive character were not, however, private family inventions, but features of a much wider moral vocabulary. Ideals such as the unity of thought and action involved standards to be followed in social and political as well as domestic circum-stances. From this perspective they reflect that search for synthesis which was a powerful influence on nineteenth-century ways of thinking. In both their Hegelian and Christian formulations such ideals paraphrase the belief that philosophy must at the same time be a philosophy of life.

Construed as an ideal, the unity of thought and action is not unproblematic. What is involved in living life as a whole? Does it require that ideals are followed in theory *and* practice? If so, is a religious believer, for example, any less a believer because he or she does not attend religious services? Questions such as these raise obvious difficulties and we can find these and others of their kind in Collingwood's writings, but they do not go to the conceptual heart of the matter. Unity of thought and action may be understood as an ideal, but it is, more importantly, a philosophical problem. In its own terms there is a strong sense in which this must be true, but it is also the case when we think about it in terms other than its own. Why must thought and action be conceived as a unity? Why do they have to be thought about in this way at all? Might there not be better arguments which show them to be distinct? How Collingwood confronted these questions is very much the story of his early thinking. What answers did he reject and how did he develop the strategies of thought that characterize his mature philosophy?

Between 1910 and 1924 when *Speculum Mentis* was published Collingwood's critical thought proceeded *pari passu* both with the development of his positive ideas and his receptivity to the influence of Continental philosophy, in particular, Italian idealism. In these years Collingwood gradually came to identify the nature of the philosophical problems that worried him. The 'big' problem was how to find a satisfactory 'rapprochement' (*A*, p. 77), between philosophy, history and practice. The fact that Collingwood chose this way of speaking is revealing because it shows how the search for synthesis between different forms of experience or different aspects of life became his dominant philosophical aspiration. Thus, his work in this period of his life is noticeable by its alertness to the close relations between activities which seem distinct. So Collingwood's weather eye was constantly kept open for points of fusion between, for example, his extensive, detailed and highly practical historical investigation of the archaeology of Roman Britain and his philosophy of history. In this, as in many of Collingwood's enquiries, a grasp of practice precedes the formulation of theory.

In Collingwood's critical thought one doctrine in particular was subject to the full force of his attack. Realism was Collingwood's philosophical *bête noire*; it was, as he put it, 'the undischarged bankrupt of modern philosophy' (*A*, p. 45). He conducted his campaign against it on three interconnected fronts. First, the central proposition of realism that knowing makes no difference to what is known commits (in Collingwood's view), the elementary error of assuming that which it claims to deny. Realism involves knowing what it has already defined as not known. The sins which Collingwood heaps at the door of realism as a result of the identification of this flaw (if flaw it is) are manifold. In restricting discussion of knowledge to relatively simple cases – 'this is a doormat', or 'this is a red rose', to use Collingwood's own examples (*A*, p. 26) – realism ignores the active, creative and inherently complex character of knowing. Just as wilfully, in Collingwood's judgement, realism is blind to the extent to which the very possibility of thinking depends upon the possession of a shared stock of concepts, in other words, a common vocabulary.

The second front of Collingwood's attack on realism concerns its implications for moral philosophy. Realism dogmatically equates knowledge with scientific knowledge and so reduces moral beliefs to the status of private, psychological impulses. Realism renders unintelligible any possible conception of a common good and, thus, divides philosophy from life.

Collingwood continued his assault on realism on a third front – the nature of its account of history. Here Collingwood's fire proved so effective in destroying realist arguments that it was to take a vital strategic importance in the advance of his own. Realism, Collingwood argued, is completely incapable of understanding history. Historical knowledge concerns the past – that which no longer exists. Since, in the realist view, knowledge is a matter of simple apprehension, historical knowledge is impossible because there can be nothing to apprehend. In its failure to comprehend history realism travesties history, its connection with practice and the operation of knowledge itself. For Collingwood, historical knowledge is found in the practice of the historian's craft. It reveals the historian asking the right questions in the right order. Likewise, self-understanding is, in part, historical under-standing. We grasp who we are by coming to see how we have come to be who we are. Similarly, the logic of question and answer is the model which tells us most about the activity of knowing. Knowledge is not propo-sitional, but interrogative.

By these means Collingwood subjected realism to fierce criticism, but in arriving at his own solutions to the problems that realism so completely failed to address he did not proceed unaided. The publication of his trans-lation of Croce's *The Philosophy of Giambattista Vico* in 1913 eloquently identifies the main influences on his thought in this period. Collingwood was receptive to Vico's ideas because they linked the creative development of mind with history in a manner that was impossible in realist terms. History, in Vico's view, is not a matter of the acceptance or rejection of 'authorities', but of interpre-tation based on the active questioning of the historian. Vico's notion of the mind unfolding through the historical life of individuals and societies held obvious attractions for a Collingwood dissatisfied with realism, but what Vico's insight lacked was a persuasive account of the logic of this operation.

Realism was held by Collingwood to be responsible for world views such as positivism and materialism which threatened civilization by infecting it with error. It became clear to Collingwood that the unity of the mind, falsely disrupted by realism and demanded by Vico's historical sensitivity, needed philosophical explanation. It was this search for a logic appropriate to the unity of mind that drew Collingwood to Italian idealism. The idea of the mind unfolding itself dialectically through its main categories offered Collingwood precisely the notion of ordered unity that realism lacked. However, Collingwood's immersion in Italian idealism, although deep, was never total. He borrowed critically from the thought of its main proponents – Croce, Gentile and de Ruggiero. As a consequence, he was influenced by them in different ways and to different degrees. In his thinking about the relation between philosophy and history, for example, he refined and qualified their views, imposing his own arguments on their ways of thinking. Indeed, in some areas, the effects of Italian idealism paralleled influences closer to home. T. H. Green, for example, can be counted as a mentor of Collingwood's early thinking on social freedom, on Christianity, and the practical value of philosophy.

Collingwood's rejection of realism came with his realization that its neglect of history and practice was not accidental; it was an essential part of its philosophical failure. But what should we make of Collingwood's realization that philosophy, history and practice are, in some sense, inextricably linked? Or, to ask the same question in more general terms, what should we make of Collingwood's argument that no aspect of mind/life is separable from any other? Is this what the unity of the mind involves?

While the idea of the unity of the mind is present in Collingwood's *Religion and Philosophy* (1916), its more complete and ornate expression is to be found in *Speculum Mentis* (1924) in which Collingwood argued that philosophy reasserts the unity of mind through the ordered elucidation of its constituent forms – art, religion, science, history and philosophy itself. During the First World War Collingwood worked in the Intelligence Division of the Admiralty. In this period, and after his return to Oxford, the nature of philosophy and history, theory and practice, and the idea of a rapprochement between them, continued to preoccupy him. Indeed, Collingwood's life's work can be plausibly described as the attempt to discover the unity between these broad bands of thought.

In the decade following the publication of *Speculum Mentis* Collingwood put forward many of his most characteristic and controversial ideas. In the philosophy of history he formulated the doctrines of reconstruction, incapsulation and re-enactment to explain how historical knowledge is both possible and essential to self-understanding. Collingwood's analysis of historical evidence, the logic of question and answer, and his notion of human activity as purposive gradually took shape in this period – a time when his extensive archaeological investigations were prompting his re-examination of the nature of history.

In the philosophy of religion, too, a typically Collingwoodian way of thinking was becoming apparent. Faith and reason are not irreconcileable, but mutually supporting; Christianity being the institutional and doctrinal embodiment of the reasonableness of religious belief. Also in political philosophy Collingwood's own brand of philosophical liberalism was taking a more substantial form. Here again we can see Collingwood's philosophical instincts encouraging him to search for unity. In this case, the looked for rapprochement is between morality and politics: his solution was to ground political action in a theory of practical reason.

Over a number of years Collingwood had reflected on the nature of philosophical method. Such reflections were integral to Collingwood's thinking because his attempt to distinguish the logical territory of art, religion, science and history requires a clear account of the standpoint from which such distinctions are made. *An Essay on Philosophical Method* (1933) was the outcome of these investigations. Arguably, it is Collingwood's most systematic work and in elegance of style bears comparison with *Speculum Mentis*, although the view of philosophical method Collingwood defends in *An Essay* is more considered and complex.

As a result of his chronic overwork Collingwood's health first began to deteriorate in 1930. Characteristically, he continued to drive himself hard. The philosophy of nature (published posthumously as *The Idea of Nature* 1945), and the task of revising his popular book, *Roman Britain* (first published 1923, revised and corrected 1932 and 1934), both occupied his time in the mid-1930s. However, his major work at this time was on the philosophy of history. He intended, first, an historical account of the emergence of the modern idea of history, and, second, a philosophical account of the differentiae of historical knowledge (published posthumously as *The Idea of History* 1946, revised edition with additional material 1993).

During 1937 Collingwood wrote *The Principles of Art* (1938) – his most important work in aesthetics. While traces of Crocean influence can be detected, the arguments are very much Collingwood's own. He develops two theories of art – an expression theory in which it is claimed that the distinctive feature of art is the expression of emotion, and an ideal theory in which it is claimed that the work of art originates as an idea in the artist's mind. In developing these theories, Collingwood draws a series of valuable distinctions between art and craft, representation, magic and amusement, in the course of which he is led into discussions of the nature of language, community and culture.

In February 1938 while working on the proofs of *The Principles of Art* Collingwood suffered the first in a series of progressively more damaging strokes. The mood in which he approached his last writings, therefore, was one of urgency. Such intimations of personal mortality could not be ignored. Neither could he stand aside from his perception of more public disintegration. In his sense of foreboding at the first signs of the Second World War Collingwood was not, of course, alone and his diagnosis of it as reflecting a spiritual as well as a political malaise was a commonly held view. Like many intellectuals Collingwood saw the War as resulting from the collusion of liberalism with its enemies. Appeasement, in Collingwood's terms, was not simply ill-advised as a policy; it was a clear indication of how enfeebled liberalism had become, of how it had lost confidence in its intellectual foundations and way of life.

What Collingwood saw during the mid-1930s was a liberal civilization destroying itself from within. In part his decision in the spring of 1938 to write his *Autobiography* reflects his attempt to reorganize his life while his health allowed him to do so, but it is also a testimony to his determination to restore liberalism's self-belief. Collingwood, therefore, demanded 'a philosophy that should be a weapon' (*A*, p. 153).

The civilization at risk here is an inherited liberal culture and the problem which Collingwood addresses with great urgency and intensity in his later writings is how such a culture can defend itself when it has nothing but its own vocabulary to fall back on. If a liberal culture is historically transient, dependent on the wills of its members rather than grounded in the idea of reason or a universal human nature, how can it protect itself against its enemies except by using its own rhetoric? This relativist difficulty arises directly from the doctrines that Collingwood was formulating at this time. If, as Collingwood argues in *An Essay on Metaphysics* (1940), the logical efficacy of the absolute presuppositions on which a liberal culture rests is independent of their being true, dependent only on their being presupposed, then how can such a culture assert the worth of its own ideals except through its own self-descriptions of them? It might be thought that in developing this argument Collingwood has succeeded only in playing into his opponents' hands. In these terms his attempt to forge philosophy as a weapon guarantees neither its truth nor its effectiveness.

It is Collingwood's view, nevertheless, that a civilization under threat can remain safe only so long as it maintains its *belief* that its 'form of life' (*EM*, p. 140) is worth living, but in Collingwood's later way of speaking there is no truth outside the boundaries of such a 'form of life' to which it can turn for support. No ultimate grounding exists immune from historical change, no bedrock of certainty to which appeal can be made when opposing practices collide.

Collingwood's later struggle with the idea that systems of belief do not depend on any ultimate realist foundations external to them is strikingly modern. His autobiographical reconstruction of his philosophical dissatisfaction with realism is of contemporary relevance, too, because it charts the relativist dangers attendant on construing the logic of question and answer as the main alternative to propositional logic.

That Collingwood writes self-consciously as a philosopher, historian and liberal serves only to sharpen the dilemmas he engages with in his later writings. How can philosophy identify, let alone remedy, the epidemic of irrationalism which Collingwood claims has infected the polity unless philosophy has a special immunity which is derived independently of the polity itself? Either a liberal culture retains some capacity for the clear-sighted identification of the disease which afflicts it or philosophy has a role in relation to practice which is logically distinguishable from the culture which surrounds it and which is exemplified in its own distinct methods and procedures.

In this respect Collingwood's preoccupation with the unity of thought and action is not abandoned in the later writings, but reappears in them as the attempt to discover a secure rapprochement between philosophy and history, theory and practice. In this search Collingwood envisages a crucial role for metaphysics. Historical knowledge, Collingwood argues, is not simply the preserve of professional historians. It is far too important for that. Historical knowledge is more like a condition of understanding than the demarcation of an intellectual terrain. In this sense, historical knowledge is self-knowledge because it informs both personal and social identity. It also represents a process of conceptual change in which systems of belief gain, or cease to have, a hold over us. How, then, can a liberal society which aspires to justice defend its ideals except by giving a philosophical restatement of them? In his final works Collingwood takes it upon himself to do precisely that.

What is noticeable about Collingwood's last writings is an unmistakeable change of tone. In such texts as *An Essay on Metaphysics* Collingwood's style becomes increasingly polemical. Analytical philosophy, for example, is denounced for its failure to see the practical consequences of its claim to moral neutrality. Psychology is berated as a jargon-filled pseudo-science. Both are vilified for their disregard of action and of the need to discover through thought the presuppositions of civilized living. Some themes remain constant, however. In their concern with metaphysics as that form of thinking through which a society becomes conscious of its deepest moral and intellectual beliefs Collingwood's last writings do not depart significantly from his earliest preoccupation with the unity of thought and action. This preoccupation is clearly evident, even though the tone of the last writings is sharper, and they are more engaged politically and more revealing about the philosophical difficulties involved in providing liberalism with a convincing intellectual lifeline.

It is difficult to know anything of Collingwood's last years without sensing the turbulent nature of his life at this time. In the spring of 1938 he began his *Autobiography* – a reconstruction of his mental life as a movement from detached to committed intellectual. In the summer of the same year we find him sailing single-handed in his yacht, *Zenocrate*, intending to put his health to the test, and, after having weathered a gale in the Channel, feeling sufficiently convinced of his recovery to continue the philosophical project he set himself to complete. In October 1938 Collingwood embarked on a voyage to Java during which he wrote *An Essay on Metaphysics*, but before sailing he invited the archaeologist, R. P. Wright, to prepare his material on Roman inscriptions for publication. In almost every vacation since the death in 1919 of his distinguished predecessor as authority on Roman Britain, F. R. Haverfield, Collingwood had steadily accumulated a vast amount of evidence through excavation and enquiry. In 1938 he came to realize that he would not be able to publish this alone. Archaeology was displaced by philosophy. While Collingwood gave Wright guidance after 1938, he came to see that his priorities must be with philosophy.

This shift in emphasis could not entail a neglect of history. *The Principles of History* (unpublished in its original form) was started at this time and, although it was to remain uncompleted, it is clear that Collingwood intended it to have a considerable presence in his later writings. In September 1939 Collingwood revised the manuscript of *The Idea of Nature* (published posthumously 1945) and completed further work in the philosophy of history. In the early summer of 1939 Collingwood clearly felt the need to take stock. His *Essay on Metaphysics* and *Autobiography* were safely completed.

Ahead lay the work to be done on *The New Leviathan*, his major contribution to political philosophy. So we can surmise that for Collingwood the invitation to join a party of Oxford undergraduates on a cruise to Greece came at exactly the right time. It offered a temporary respite from ill-health and also from the constant need to write against the clock. At the very least, it gave Collingwood a fresh perspective on a world preparing for war, and, through contact with the intelligent young, an opportunity for spiritual renewal. The book that emerged from the excursion to the Aegean was Collingwood's sea-diary, *The First Mate's Log* (1940).

Whilst *The First Mate's Log*, which Collingwood himself described as 'small beer', contains hints of some of the loadbearing doctrines of *The New Leviathan* it does no more than that. For the appropriate context of *The New Leviathan* we should look to Collingwood's own intellectual biography because the arguments of Collingwood's last book are set by the account of morality he developed over many years. As published, *The New Leviathan* is divided into four parts – Man, Society, Civilization and Barbarism. In Parts One and Two Collingwood elucidates his theory of mind and ethical system. Part Three on civilization reflects his long-standing interest in what promotes and what endangers civilized existence between individuals and societies. Part Four is an examination of barbarism – its nature and threat. This fourth part of *The New Leviathan* is the briefest section of the book. It was completed between June and August 1941 and its brevity is, in large measure, due to the further severe stroke which Collingwood suffered in the early January of that year. It is the only part of the work whose defects were explicitly attributed by Collingwood to illness. The Preface was added in January 1942 and the book was published later that year.

In *The New Leviathan* Collingwood resolved to build on Hobbes's recognition that in political philosophy when faced by 'those that content, on the one side far too great liberty and on the other side far too much authority, 'tis hard to pass between the points of both unwounded' (Hobbes, *Leviathan*, Dedication). However, the philosophical methods used by Collingwood to avoid this fate reveal a clear departure from Hobbes. Collingwood's philosophy of mind is not Hobbes's, and the contractarian procedure Collingwood deployed in his derivation of the political order is a highly modified one. It emphasizes the need for political education as much as the presence of agreement in the construction of a civil order.

The New Leviathan was Collingwood's last book – the last expression of his determination to make his philosophical voice heard above the sound of war. We know that Collingwood intended his last works to make up a series. The *Essay on Metaphysics* was to be the companion volume to the *Essay on Philosophical Method* under the general title, *Philosophical Essays*. The manuscript of *The Principles of History* was to accompany *The Principles of Art* under the rubric *Philosophical Principles*. The manuscripts of *The Idea of Nature* and *The Idea of History* were to be published together as volumes one and two of *Studies in the History of Ideas*. This aim does not, however, reflect an interest in intellectual neatness for its own sake. Rather it is an expression of Collingwood's deep concern for the unity of mind, systematically understood. After the completion of *The New Leviathan* there is no evidence of Collingwood continuing with his planned multiple series, or of starting new work. To a degree, therefore, we do not possess Collingwood's works as he intended them to be published. In 1935 Collingwood was appointed Waynflete Professor of Metaphysical Philosophy at Oxford, a position from which he resigned in 1941. His health deteriorated rapidly at this time and in late spring 1942 he moved to the Lake District, to the house left him by his father. He was seriously ill for the last few months of his life, and he died at Coniston on 9 January 1943.

The prominence Collingwood gave to discussion of political life is unmistakeable in his later writing. As his extensive manuscript material on folklore and fairy tales (deposited in the Bodleian Library, Oxford) testifies, he lost none of his enthusiasm for the byways of thought, for the arcane or the not sufficiently noticed. But in the more serious terms of the political engagement of the philosopher and of the capacity of politics to construct a world which satisfies liberal needs Collingwood's special attention to politics is clear. It is also the case, however, that Collingwood's explorations took him to the limits of politics. Consider, for example, Collingwood's treatment of the concept of civility in *The New Leviathan*. What this illustrates is a determination not to concede the relativist implications of his view that meaning is dependent on a specific historical context or 'form of life'. Civility is to be elucidated not simply as a guiding norm of existing social practices, but as an ideal to which such practices represent a more or less adequate approximation. The loss of a concept like civility is, therefore, more like losing a general condition of human life than a particular social convention. It is possibly for this reason that in *The New Leviathan* justice takes second place to civility as politics does to civilization. To this extent, Collingwood's version of philosophical liberalism parts company with the dominant forms of it today.

Collingwood's acute awareness of the boundaries of politics encourages him to ask what human beings fall back on when politics fails. His late article, 'Fascism and Nazism' (1940), reveals just how extensively Collingwood's final philosophical manifesto was dependent on a set of specifically Christian beliefs. Religion is at the centre of civilized living. Take it away and the will to form decent and resilient liberal political communities is lost.

In his *Autobiography* Collingwood demanded that philosophy be understood as a weapon. This is not a rhetorical flourish. Rather it represents a dramatic re-shaping of Collingwood's earlier claim, made in *Speculum Mentis*, that 'all thought exists for the sake of action' (*SM*, p. 15); a society's world is its language and if this is corrupted the way it acts will be similarly affected and the confidence it has in its ideals undermined. There is no doubt that Collingwood took a pessimistic view of the capacity of liberalism to revitalize itself – 'in so far as consciousness is corrupted, the very wells of truth are poisoned. Intellect can build nothing firm. Moral ideals are castles in the air. Political and economic systems are mere cobwebs. Even common sanity and bodily health are no longer secure' (*PA*, pp. 289–90). To redeem this bleak situation Collingwood thought of philosophy as transformative, of himself as the self-appointed cleanser of modernity's Augean stables.

It is easy to see why Collingwood's conception of philosophy as a weapon implies transfiguration. There would be little point in thinking of it in this way if using philosophy in practical argument and debate left the world unchanged. Philosophy does not leave everything as it is. But from what standpoint does philosophy begin its work if we have nothing to fall back on other than historically mutable forms of life?

Consider, again, Collingwood's understanding of civility as an ideal. This implies that not anything can count as a civil relationship, but it insists, in equal measure, that civility requires historical expression if it is to be more than simply a set of abstract rules. Ideals *can* be formulated by philosophy, Collingwood seems to say, but they would be redundant if human beings were blind to their temporal nature. Nevertheless, between the philosophical aspiration and the historical reality there remains a considerable tension.

Earlier I spoke of conversing with Collingwood. One of the features of philosophy which stimulates conversation is that what one philosopher sees as a solution another sees as a problem. What one counts as evidence of understanding another views as a reason for thinking confusion still reigns. In Collingwood's case, many of his most notable and distinctive ideas concerning, say, philosophy as self-knowledge, or the historical character of knowing, invite just such a response. They do so in part because Collingwood's hermeneutical stress on the importance of self-understanding hints at relativism and this touches a contemporary philosophical nerve.

Chapter 2
PHILOSOPHY AND METHOD

When Thrasymachus in the *Republic* complains that Socrates is trying to trick him with fancy arguments he seems to speak for all those who find philosophy a puzzling and mysterious activity. Thrasymachus thinks that his view of the nature of ruling and its connection with justice is so obviously true that anyone would agree with it, but Socrates through argument makes him doubt it. What is it about philosophical thinking, Thrasymachus might be taken as asking, which raises it above trickery?

One way of tackling this question is to say that philosophy possesses certain general features which distinguish it from adjacent modes of thought. Another way is to explain the distinctive methods that philosophy uses. A different way, again, is to identify the special subject matter of philosophy. Grasp these things, a Socrates-like philosopher might say to a Thrasymachus-like complainant, and you can begin philosophy. You have acquired philosophy's methods and you have understood its subject matter so now you can begin to practise it. Your difficulty arose because you thought of yourself as an outsider – now you have been initiated you can join the conversation.

On the face of it this response seems clear enough. If the issue is the nature of philosophy then it is to philosophy that we must go for enlightenment, and, yet, when Thrasymachus-like enquirers do turn to philosophy they find that philosophy doubts the things they most take for granted. The reality of the external world, the existence of other minds, the force of our moral obligations, have all been subject to philosophical doubt. What is the point, then, in going to philosophy for an explanation of itself when it invents the doubts which give its arguments their rationale? From the perspective of our Thrasymachus-like critic it looks as if philosophy is being judge and jury in its own case. Philosophy plays the game and philosophy sets the rules. So, it *is* nothing more than trickery – Thrasymachus was right all along.

Is there any way of reaching an understanding of philosophy which avoids this difficulty? Is there a way of thinking that is just peculiar to philosophy? Collingwood spends a great deal of effort wrestling with these questions. He does so, in part, because he wishes to explain to non-philosophers what philosophy is and what it can achieve; in part, because he wishes to distinguish philosophy from, say, science or religion, and also because he wishes to take philosophy beyond the naive conception of it he found in realism.

In thinking that philosophy must give an account of itself Collingwood is not, of course, alone. The idea that philosophy is a quest for its own self-definition is longstanding in the history of philosophy. This is not, however, an enterprise which can be conducted uncontroversially since the terms in which the identity of philosophy is expressed are themselves open to debate. Nevertheless, the questions with which philosophy is concerned do seem to share a number of specific characteristics and Collingwood states what he takes these to be.

For Collingwood, philosophy is thinking about thinking. It is thought at one degree removed from its object. In other words, philosophical thought is reflective thought. Since human understanding is diverse in nature and object, what philosophy reflects on varies. It may be the formation of our beliefs or our claims to knowledge. It may be the nature of the physical world and the scientific laws which govern it. Our ability to make moral judgements, to find some objects beautiful and others ugly, to form political communities, to hold religious beliefs – all these may be the subjects of philosophical reflection. In each case, Collingwood argues, it is the business of philosophy to draw out the logical character of the experience under investigation. Philosophy elucidates in logical form what moral activity, for example, seems in some sense to take for granted in order to be what it is. In so doing, philosophy raises questions which moral activity is unable to raise.

At this point, however, we encounter a difficulty. If philosophy is concerned with the logical differentia of knowledge claims then, surely, its investigations are merely piecemeal, unconnected one with another. Collingwood denies this. Philosophy may be second order thinking, but it is not simply parasitic on the first order experience it seeks to understand. What, then, does philosophy bring of its own to the activities it wishes to clarify? Philosophy, Collingwood argues, brings systematic thought. While acknowledging that no philosophical system can ever be final Collingwood insists nevertheless that no one part of philosophy can be pursued independently of its implications for any other part. This means that philosophy must be conducted systematically, not simply to satisfy the demands of consistency, or to notice connections between, say, ethics and aesthetics, but to elucidate the logical character of different forms of experience and the relationships between them. Philosophical thinking is methodical thinking, but it is also thinking systematically which means making explicit the principles already implicit in experience.

Two difficulties arise at this stage. In attempting to think systematically about the world, philosophy, in Collingwood's view, seems to commit itself to picturing the world as a system. Philosophy on this model is a kind of super-science which tells us how the world is ordered and how our ways of ordering it are related. But is it possible to map the world in the way that this conception of philosophy requires? The business of philosophy is more with the world's detail, with life seen in its particularity rather than its totality. In other words, it is not possible for philosophy to legislate concerning the boundaries of, say, religion and science if these depend on the changing conceptions of religious believers and scientists themselves. Furthermore, it must surely be the case that for philosophy to render the world intelligible in its totality it must stand outside the world. But how, then, can philosophy speak to those *in* the world? Philosophy, Collingwood tells us, makes explicit what artists and scientists, for example, know only implicitly, but this must mean that artists and scientists are unable to understand their places in the world as philosophy does. In the face of such disparities of self-understanding the philosophical quest for an account of the world as an integrated whole is surely questionable.

It is open to Collingwood to resist this conclusion by making his account of philosophy's tasks less ambitious. He would then argue that no philosophical system can be final because the account each offers of life as a whole is simply a way of generating new problems for philosophy to solve. Philosophical solutions are interesting only insofar as they point to new problems. A system that was completely harmonious with itself would mark the death of philosophy.

So, in Collingwood's view, what is it that keeps philosophy alive? Philosophy thrives when it treats its object as activity. Whether this is moral, artistic or religious, what occupies philosophy is uncovering the criterion according to which each activity evaluates itself. Since human activities are not sets of behavioural movements lacking any capacity for self-analysis and judgement, they can be understood only from within. Standards of self-assessment are internal to the practices concerned. In grasping this, Collingwood is saying, philosophy comes closer to the nature of morality, for example, than psychology does which construes it through its own descriptive categories.

Collingwood's insistence that philosophy takes its starting point to be activity, rather than event or substance, echoes his belief that philosophy should not depart too far from experience. No philosophy can flourish if it neglects the ways human activities are actually undertaken. Aesthetics demands an appreciation of what is involved in painting a picture or writing a novel. The philosophy of science would be directionless without a clear sense of how scientists work and what convinces them that their experiments are on the right lines. Understanding of this kind is essential, Collingwood believes, if philosophy is not to become self-enclosed, but philosophical reflection must also be distinctive in that it brings something of its own to the activities it seeks to explain.

Collingwood thinks of the distinctiveness of philosophy in terms of: its aim which is to show why our experience must be as it is; its character which comprises the criteria which enable it to proceed through self-criticism and self-assessment; and its method. In attempting to say why our experience must be as it is, philosophy, in Collingwood's view, is thinking of a categorical kind. Such thinking does not simply ask, for example, how we can give an historical account of the past, but whether we can think of human life as historical in character at all. This question history is unable to answer because it is a question about the ultimate nature of things. It is this that makes it a question for philosophy. Similarly, science may be understood as a procedure whereby laws or law-like generalizations are constructed on the basis of observation and experiment. To ask by what conceptual token such evidence is to count as evidence is, however, to go beyond science to philosophy. As with the question – is there a first cause? – it is a question science cannot answer.

But why should we think that a question science cannot answer is a question that philosophy can? The idea that philosophy can tell us about the ultimate nature of the world is one that many philosophers rightly regard with suspicion. What kind of questions, we might ask Collingwood, are the ultimate questions with which philosophy is supposed to deal? In assuming that ultimate questions are actually questions in much the same way as non-ultimate ones, philosophy is doing no more than manufacturing its own difficulties. On the other hand, a denial that ultimate questions are its special preserve seems to put itself out of a job.

Collingwood's association with the idea of philosophy as a science of ultimate questions arises, in part, from his early affinities with idealism – a term Collingwood disliked when used about himself, although he was not averse to using it about others – but it stems, too, from his onslaught on analytical philosophy which he described as 'that numerous and frightful offspring of propositional logic out of illiteracy, the various attempts at a "logical language", beginning with the pedantry of the textbooks about "reducing a proposition to logical form", and ending, for the present, in the typographical jargon of *Principia Mathematica*' (*A*, pp. 35–6 fn 1).

If the world cannot be made transparent to us through the terms employed by analytical philosophy then what does Collingwood propose as a viable alternative? We know already that for Collingwood philosophy is an autonomous activity of thought, distinct from both the exact and the empirical sciences. It is capable of self-reflection in a way that they are not, and it is, therefore, uniquely placed to formulate and answer questions about what is necessary and universal in human experience. Philosophy, in this picture of it, distinguishes the ways by which we understand the world and shows how they are related. Art, science and history, for example, involve conceptually distinct vocabularies, judiciously observed by philosophy. Collingwood's alternative to analytical philosophy is philosophy as conceptual self-exploration – 'philosophical writing (is) essentially a confession, a search by the mind for its own failings and an attempt to remedy them by recognizing them' (*EPM*, p. 210).

The image of philosophical thinking as a confession can be misleading if it distracts us from seeing that the world philosophy attempts to be clear about is not that of a single self repetitiously searching for its faults, but a common possession. Collingwood does not aspire to the Platonic condition of making the world fit for philosophy, but he does wish to give philosophy a privileged role. Among our many different ways of thinking about the world philosophy alone decodes their vocabularies to us. Philosophy alone monitors thought for its misrepresentations and in remedying them revitalizes itself. The point of philosophy, as Collingwood understands it, is not the construction of a technical language – this relegates philosophy, as he puts it himself, to a 'futile parlour game' (*A*, p. 50) – but the discovery of self-knowledge.

What gives philosophy its title to this exalted status? Collingwood's answer is largely an explanation of the method he takes to be appropriate to this conception of philosophy. Whether or not the method is chosen simply to fit the conception is debatable, but what is clear is that while the account of philosophical method Collingwood formulates in *An Essay on Philosophical Method* (1933) grew out of his early lectures on moral philosophy, it expands the main argument of *Speculum Mentis* (1924) *and* anticipates the logic of practical reason developed in *The New Leviathan* (1942). In other words, it is a method which is at work throughout Collingwood's mature philosophical thinking. I will, first, outline its essential features and, second, consider its weaknesses.

Collingwood described *An Essay on Philosophical Method* as his 'best book in matter' and his 'only book' in style (*A*, p. 118). One reason for this judgement is the importance to Collingwood of the conception of philosophical method he developed there. Philosophy, Collingwood argues, does not proceed by imitating the methods of the sciences, both empirical and exact. Scientific explanations involve the classification of objects in terms of genus and species, so reaching a precise and exhaustive account of their nature. In philosophy it is not possible to work in this manner. In scientific explanation an individual instance of one species cannot also be an instance of another species of the same genus, but in philosophy concepts behave differently. In an exact science like mathematics, for example, to know how a concept is defined is to know the concept; not to know the definition is to be ignorant of the concept. In philosophy, however, concepts do not have this character. Someone ignorant of the various attempts to define justice, say, may still know what justice is.

One reason why definition has a limited role to play in philosophy is that it neglects the ways concepts have a bearing on each other. It is possible to see one concept under the aspect or rubric of another, so some good things are also pleasant, some just things are also expedient. Similarly, concepts overlap in the sense that characteristics of one may be found in the operation of another. Philosophical concepts lack the exclusivity which is a feature of science and philosophical method must be adapted in ways which reflect this.

It is a key feature of philosophical thinking, as Collingwood understands it, that the concepts it deals with are not explicable by the methods of classification appropriate to science. Why should this be so? Collingwood answers by considering the commonly expressed view in ethics that virtue can be divided into four kinds – temperance, courage, wisdom and justice. Virtue is the genus of which the kinds of virtue are species, but these species do not only exhibit differences in kind. They also reveal differences in degree, so temperance, for example, may be counted less virtuous than courage. But, Collingwood asks, how can this be? Either temperance is a species of the genus virtue, or it is not. If it is, it is so completely; if it is not, then the degree to which it is not makes no difference. Collingwood's solution to this difficulty is the idea of a scale of forms. From this perspective, virtue differs both in kind and degree. As such it is not possible to grade virtue by reference to differences of degree alone. Neither, as we have seen, is it possible to separate completely differences of degree from differences in kind. As a specification of virtue, temperance, in this picture, satisfies the requirements of the kind of virtue it is *and* to that degree embodies virtue in general, but it is also distinguishable from courage on the same grounds. Courage, too, satisfies the requirements of the kind of virtue it is, but is also embodies virtue in general to a greater degree than temperance and, hence, tells us more about what virtue in general is. In this way, Collingwood is driven by what seems to be the logic of his own arguments to identify the idea of the scale of forms as that method which distinguishes philosophical thinking –

> If in philosophical thought every difference of kind is also a difference of degree, the specifications of a philosophical concept are bound to form a scale; and in this scale their common essence is bound to be realized differentially in degree as well as differentially in kind. (*EPM*, p. 77)

Understanding concepts in terms of a scale of forms gives philosophy an altogether more ambitious task than noticing resemblances between them. Analysis of concepts on the basis of a scale of forms is intended by Collingwood to reveal overlap and hierarchy. Concepts do not stand as autonomous units to each other, but as overlapping in a progressively developing series, each stage of which is related to its predecessor as advanced is to lower. The logical movement from one form to another is not that of a causal sequence, but of an overlapping chain in which each successive stage both confirms and extends the one before.

In speaking in this way about the method he considers appropriate in philosophy Collingwood is, in effect, encouraging us to ask what the method can achieve. His replies confirm our expectations, although they do not always satisfy them. Collingwood refers to the scale of forms as the only true method in philosophy. He uses it consistently and extensively in his thought to elucidate the logic of a variety of concepts – different kinds and degrees of experience, of knowledge, of reality, of goodness, of action, of virtue and, indeed, of philosophy itself. Philosophical thinking in practice and in its historical development can be construed as a process in which new phases of argument continually modify and extend those which precede them. Collingwood's notion of the scale of forms seems, then, to be especially well-suited to his conception of philosophy as a uniquely self-referential activity. This is because it offers philosophy a way of thinking about itself as the paramount process of self-discovery, free from the presumptive influence of science. Philosophical thinking arises from experience. The scale of forms provides Collingwood with the method for thinking about different forms of experience as reflecting neither distinct mental faculties nor divisions in experience itself. It allows him, in other words, to re-assert his claim that the human mind is active, integrated and transformative in character.

Should we be convinced by these arguments? Consider two of the ways in which Collingwood deploys his conception of philosophical method. Look, first, at his analysis of different forms of human experience in *Speculum Mentis*. Read as an application of method, Collingwood's analysis aims to show that the forms of mental life are systematically related to each other as stages in the development of rational self-consciousness. Art, religion, science, history and philosophy are construed as forms of knowledge in which all the faculties are engaged. Each claims the authority to speak truthfully about the world; each form is, therefore, potentially a rival to every other. Collingwood argues that there is no way of examining these knowledge claims from without. There is no external or neutral standpoint from which an investigation can start. Each form of experience must be understood from within. From their own perspectives, however, forms of experience are unstable creatures because each elevates its own appropriate self-understanding to an inappropriate picture of the whole. To overcome this, Collingwood resolves to show how the forms of experience are linked on a scale of forms, each form both a presupposition of its successor and an advance on its predecessor. In this way, art shades into religion, religion into science, and so on. Philosophy, however, is different because it is only through its methods that this conclusion can be reached. Philosophical understanding enables us to think of mental life as a unity. It is the key to self-knowledge, but what does philosophy discover when the key is turned?

On Collingwood's own admission philosophy does not stand to art, religion, etc., as cartography does to virgin ground. Philosophy does not provide new ways of mapping forms of experience because there are no independent territories to map. Each form perceives the world from its own standpoint, and, therefore, contributes to that degree to self-understanding. What philosophy discovers, Collingwood argues, contra realism, is that truth resides in the worlds the mind constructs for itself. What philosophy finally reveals is that 'the mind…realizes that it has been not exploring an external world but tracing its own lineaments in a mirror' (*SM*, p. 316).

Rudyard Kipling is not normally counted as an acute philosophical critic, but it is hard to disagree with his comment on this conclusion that 'the *dénouement* is that there isn't any *dénouement* – only deliquescence' (*RK*, p. 553). It is perfectly possible to think about art, science, history and philosophy as each giving their own answers to the different questions they raise about the world without suggesting that they are related or that any one of them describes the world better than any other. Similarly, we can accept that these are mental activities without positing something called 'mind' which all in some sense and to some degree make manifest.

One of Collingwood's strengths in philosophy is his range; little in life that is worthy of philosophical attention escapes him, but in relation to philosophical method this strength can seem a fault. The weakness comes about because Collingwood sees philosophical method not as a way of elucidating or clarifying experience, but as imposing an order on it. Collingwood is a philosopher noted for putting practice before theory so it is odd to find him espousing a philosophical method which presumes too much about what individuals think they are doing when, for example, they paint pictures, pray in church or conduct experiments in a laboratory. Rather than allowing these activities to speak for themselves it is the logic of the scale of forms which determines how they should be understood.

Let us consider this point further by looking at a second way in which Collingwood's commitment to a particular method in philosophy influences his arguments. Thinking about concepts in terms of a scale of forms requires that we construe them not as mutually exclusive, but as both overlapping and arranged hierarchically. So Collingwood writes – 'each term…has also a double relation to its neighbours: in comparison with the one below, it is what that professes to be; in comparison with the one above, it professes to be what that is' (*EPM*, p. 87). In applying this logic to the familiar distinction in ethics between duty and expediency Collingwood claims that 'all dutiful actions are expedient, for duty as the higher specification always and necessarily reaffirms the lower; and the lower not sometimes but always partially and incompletely affirms the higher' (*EPM*, p. 91).

Now if this is meant as a description then it is surely false, so Collingwood must mean something more by it. One possibility is to read Collingwood as saying that expediency is a less adequate expression of the moral (whatever that is) than duty, but then we would need some way of testing adequacy and, in any case, this reading does not capture the full force of Collingwood's words. Alternatively, we can take his point to be that we cannot judge expediency as inferior except from the perspective of duty, but, again, this seems doubtful in itself and reflects only part of his meaning. Consider, then, a more radical interpretation. In terms of the scale of forms the relationship between duty and expediency excludes both mutual collision and mutual accommodation. To say, as Collingwood does, that 'all dutiful actions are expedient' must mean that expediency is in some sense transformed by duty so that it is not what it is alone. Acting honestly out of duty, therefore, might be said to pay; acting honestly from motives of expediency alone is not honesty at all.

But are we correct in granting Collingwood the truth of this? It may be the case that utility often points to considerations such as the quality of life which, strictly speaking, it should be incapable of explaining, but which are essential to any moral vocabulary worth the name. A considerable distance remains, nevertheless, between this and the idea that utility and the quality of life overlap so that morality appears in the latter with greater clarity and determination than in the former. Perhaps all we can say here about the relation between duty and expediency is that in addition to their more obvious collisions they also can coincide, but there is nothing in the idea of coincidence which warrants the conclusion that they overlap.

Collingwood's defence of the scale of forms can be seen as a part of the 'debris of Absolute Idealism' (*PTC*, p. 193), and in ethics, for example, it is not difficult so see how it underestimates the intransigence of fundamental conflict both within morality and between moral and non-moral points of view. Philosophical method, as Collingwood understands it, is hugely significant both in the opulent structures of thought which compose *Speculum Mentis* and the more refined and controlled arguments of the *Essay on Philosophical Method*. What part it plays in Collingwood's discussion of specific philosophical topics outside these texts is a more contentious matter. It is to these topics, starting with the philosophy of mind, that we now turn.

Chapter 3
MIND AND CONSCIOUSNESS

An anthology of twentieth-century philosophy of history which turned a blind eye to Collingwood would soon find itself ignored. The same could not be said of the philosophy of mind, and yet the issues with which it deals – the nature of mind, the mind/body and mind/world relation – are central to Collingwood's thinking. As regards *Speculum Mentis* this cannot be other than true, but it applies also to *The Principles of Art* and *The New Leviathan* where problems of the philosophy of mind figure prominently in the discussion.

Collingwood's early theorizing about the nature of mind takes place in the broad context of the view of philosophy he arrived at in *Speculum Mentis*. Here the philosophy of mind is not seen as a specialized area within philosophy, in the way we might think of the philosophy of language or the philosophy of logic, but rather as a vital component of philosophy's main task, which is to show how in knowing the world mind comes to know itself. Collingwood's early view of mind is, therefore, deeply embedded in his formative thinking about the nature of reality. The world possesses the character it does through the ways we come to know it. Art, religion, science, history and, finally, philosophy itself all represent successive stages in the development of the mind's self-knowledge. With varying degrees of logical abstractness they constitute the ways by which the mind in structuring the world comes to know itself. Philosophy through its unique recognition of this process stands as the culmi-nation of the mind's achievements and the arbiter of the territories to which art, religion, science and history lay claim. The role of mind in this undeniably idealist picture is made plain by Collingwood in the following passage:

> The mind is not one among a number of objects of knowledge, which possesses the peculiarity of being alone fully knowable: it is that which is really known in the ostensible knowing of any object whatever. In an immediate and direct way, the mind can never know itself: it can only know itself through the mediation of an external world, know that what it sees in the external world is its own reflection. Hence the construction of external worlds – works of art, religions, sciences, structures of historical fact, codes of law, systems of philosophy and so forth *ad infinitum* – is the only way by which the mind can possibly come to that self-knowledge which is its end. (*SM*, p. 315)

Responses to this project of construction will, of course, vary depending, in part, on the degree of sympathy felt for its metaphysical ambition. This ambition alone must surely separate Collingwood's schema from contemporary concerns in the philosophy of mind. For Collingwood shows little interest in the logic of mental concepts per se. *Speculum Mentis* contains hardly any analysis of thinking, feeling and perceiving independently of its own philosophical aim. Mapping the world, Collingwood argues, must reveal its unity with mind. Such a claim is certainly and beneficially distant from those theories which attempt to explain mind in individualist or subjective terms, but in its search for a truth about mind that is all-encompassing it depends upon idealist logical doctrines – the synthesis of opposites, internal relations and the holistic conception of truth; doctrines which creak under the weight Collingwood places on them. Collingwood's treatment of mind in *Speculum Mentis* is certainly less prosaic than ours, but we might reply in return that the mirror image of mind and reality with which its argument concludes reflects not a truth independently ascertained, but an uncertain and misleading metaphor.

If our appreciation of Collingwood's philosophy of mind depended solely on the doctrines of *Speculum Mentis*, then, one suspects, it would have dwindled long ago. This is another way of saying that it is in his later thinking about mind that Collingwood speaks to us more directly, in a voice less affected by the all-embracing phenomenological aims of *Speculum Mentis*. This later Collingwood, the Collingwood primarily of *The New Leviathan*, is a philosopher of mind we can listen to. He talks to us in a much more contemporary idiom. Nevertheless, there are points of continuity with his early thinking which concern not his positive doctrines about the nature of mind, but those he rejects.

Foremost among these false doctrines is realism, a point of view Collingwood found so full of error that his impeachment of it is central to the whole of his philosophical work. Realism not only fails disastrously as a theory of knowledge, but also as an account of mind. Collingwood finds it blind to that stock of shared mental concepts which makes creative questioning possible and which, indeed, may not always be transparent to the questioner. Realism pictures mental life as static, involving little more than the passive reception of crude, uninterpreted fact. Unsurprisingly in view of the general drift of Collingwood's criticism, materialist theories of mind fare no better. Understanding mind is not a matter of looking inwards towards the discovery of those elements in the brain on which our dispositions and capacities are printed and connecting them with other elements. It involves the altogether more holistic enterprise of looking outwards to those features of a public language without which the operation of our mental concepts would remain unintelligible. On the materialist view, Collingwood remarks:

> I am a kind of factory for converting wave-lengths into colours, air disturbances into sounds. (*PA*, pp. 196–7)

It is not, however, Collingwood's criticism of realism and materialism in his early philosophy of mind that makes our own thinking receptive to his voice. The doctrines of *Speculum Mentis* swing too far in the direction of idealist reduction for this, and, in any case, they are developed by Collingwood within a broadly mind/matter framework which he later completely disavows. When Collingwood writes:

> In the case of human products, indeed, we get nearer to their reality, not further away, by describing them as mental. A boot is more adequately described in terms of mind – by saying who made it and what he made it for – than in terms of matter. (*RP*, p. 93)

we see clearly how firmly the early works are wedded to this framework and this makes his later abandonment of it more astonishing and, to us, more topical.

The dualist picture of philosophical psychology which Collingwood rejects in *The New Leviathan* is a familiar one and needs little rehearsal here. Dualism sees human beings as composed of mind and body. Human behaviour is seen as bodily movement on the basis of which the mental states of others can be inferred by an analogy with one's own. The essential problem of philosophical psychology is that of explaining how mind and matter can relate when it is clear that they belong to radically different logical categories. It is this dualist paradigm which modern philosophy overturns, so erasing the philosophical problems it generates. The work of Wittgenstein and Ryle is, of course, decisive in this respect, but Collingwood, too, in his last writings, must be read as formulating substantially similar insights.

In *The New Leviathan* (2.41), he expresses his initial view bluntly. The mind/body problem is bogus. With this recognition we can discard the assumption that mind and body belong to different categories and replace it with the altogether more suggestive idea that what faces us is one thing which can be understood in different ways. Collingwood's dissolution of the mind/body problem releases him from the traditional difficulty of showing how mental and corporeal entities can be related and this, in turn, enables him to dismiss as 'old wives' tales' the various theories of their relation. If, as Collingwood recognizes, mind and body are not two different things, there is simply no point in trying to explain their interaction, whether in terms of correlative or parallel development. More importantly, Collingwood identifies the most common fable about mind and body to be the idea that the one inhabits the other in much the same way as an individual inhabits a house. In rescuing philosophical psychology from this misleading image Collingwood is refusing to be beguiled by the inner/outer picture of the mind in which subjects, through introspection, possess privileged access to their own mental states, and behaviour in the public world is thought of entirely in terms of bodily movement.

What should we make of Collingwood's own philosophy of mind? In dismantling the dualist picture Collingwood discards the inner/outer theory of the mind and with it the idea that the mental is available to its subject through introspection. The claim that human action is bodily movement caused by interior promptings of the will is also set aside. From our contemporary viewpoint such doctrines may be thought well lost, but what theory of the mind does Collingwood offer in their place? From his assertion that mind and body are not two different things but one thing looked at from different perspectives, Collingwood's philosophy of mind moves in a number of directions.

There is the attempt to follow through the assertion, present in both *Speculum Mentis* (p. 241) and *The New Leviathan* (9.16), that mind is to be understood not as substance, but activity. In *The New Leviathan* Collingwood describes the mind he wishes to explain as belonging neither to an individual nor even to a collection of individuals. Rather it is the possession of a society at a certain stage of its development. The mind to be explained is, therefore, the modern European mind and Collingwood's task is to show how it has come to be what it is and how it has generated the civilization we associate with it. To link the philosophy of mind with the mind's history would seem to suggest that what Collingwood is looking for is a genealogy of mind, and to the extent that genealogy implies logical development as opposed to merely circumstantial change, this is, indeed, what he wishes to discover. There is a difficulty here, however. Showing why x has come to be what it is, even in terms of its logical development, is not the same as showing why x *must* be the case. If we substitute for x the modern European mind then we see just how acute Collingwood's difficulty is. The historical course taken by the European mind is by no means smooth nor is its explanation beyond dispute. To think that a genealogy of mind can be as compelling as a philosophical argument is, therefore, to collapse philosophy into history rather than unite them in a form of discourse which combines the merits of each.

Mind and body, Collingwood states, are not two different things, but one thing seen under different aspects. What aspects are these and how are they related? One obvious way of looking at mind is via natural science. Understanding mind means understanding its place in nature. It means formulating law-like causal connections between thought and action, self and world. In looking at mind as matter, natural science succeeds, however, in ignoring everything that is uniquely significant about mind. Intentionality and self-reflectiveness can be accommodated only by changing the perspective. History and philosophy must be candidates in this respect, but, in Collingwood's thinking, psychology is not. As an empirical science of mind psychology's province is causation; it is concerned not with the reasons for holding a belief, but with its cause; not with the logical status of a piece of critical thinking, but its connection with some other state of affairs. Once an empirical science of mind trespasses beyond its boundaries then its errors are easily seen. 'Reasons' are confused with 'causes'; 'intentions' are confused with 'motives'; 'feelings' are confused with 'thoughts'. Now we might describe these as confusions because each involves a category mistake. Each accounts for the operation of one concept in terms which can be ascribed only to another. However, in interpreting Collingwood in this contemporary way we need to be careful. On the idealist view, forms of enquiry, such as natural science and history, are not related as competitors in pursuit of truth, but as partial visions of the whole. From the perspective of the whole there *is* no category mistake, but instead more or less adequate pictures of itself. To read Collingwood in starkly modern terms means, therefore, jettisoning much of the idealist superstructure from his thought. Against dualism Collingwood offers an account in which mental states are closely integrated one with another. To some, however, this essentially humanist picture may simply assume too much harmony in its subject to shed light on questions such as the emergence of intentionality from non-intentionality or the role of social and physical factors external to the individual in determining the content of mental beliefs.

What Collingwood expects from philosophical psychology is not simply the capacity to show why our mental states have the character they do, but also, more ambitiously, how they are logically related to each other – how, for example, sensing, tasting and feeling are connected to more demanding and complex states like desiring and choosing. Discarding Cartesianism is clearly Collingwood's first move in making progress with this project. Likewise, he is at one with Wittgenstein in asserting emphatically that the appropriate form of understanding here is not empirical.

Whatever meaning mental expressions have in language it does not consist in private mental states or processes. This means that such expressions do not predicate part of mind, or body as opposed to mind, but rather the whole person. Wittgenstein puts this point as follows – 'only of a living human being and what resembles (behaves like) a living human being can one say: it has sensations; it sees; is blind; hears; is deaf; is conscious or unconscious' (*PI*, p. 281).

Collingwood, as we have seen, understands mind as activity; activity he construes as thought, and thought in its most primitive form is consciousness. He writes, 'the essential *constituent* of mind is *consciousness* or thought (practical and theoretical) in its most rudimentary form' (*NL*, 4.18). The mysteries of mind are, then, in large measure, the mysteries of consciousness. Dissolve these, Collingwood may be taken as saying, and the mind's activities should become transparent to us. Consciousness is of the mind's essence, but feeling, Collingwood argues, stands to it as an accompaniment. This relation is not, however, one of *mere* accompaniment. Feelings are not simply the accidental companions of consciousness, but belong to it in some more fundamental way. Collingwood's philosophical method contains a number of features which reinforce this point. First, consciousness is understood to mean awareness and this means being aware *of* something. What consciousness in its most primitive form apprehends is feeling in its most primitive form. Feelings are those states of which we are, or become, conscious. Second, Collingwood draws a familiar distinction between a state in which I am conscious of something and being conscious that I am conscious of that something. The difference between these two states encourages Collingwood to speak in Hegelian fashion of levels of consciousness. Reflection on the mind's activities reveals a logical development from simple apprehension to thought of a more complex order. Third, Collingwood thinks of this development as a progressive, but not a predictable, one and this implies, in turn, the need for some account of how different levels of consciousness are related. Collingwood does not picture movement from one level to another as a process of eradication. Shifting from state A to state B does not abolish A, but incorporates it in a different form of understanding. When hunger, for example, evolves into love, hunger is not lost, but is seen as something which can be set aside. When desire, for example, develops into reason, desire is not lost, but is seen as open to qualification through reflection and judgement.

The task of philosophical psychology is, in Collingwood's view, that of compiling an inventory of mental concepts. But it is an inventory of a special kind. Starting by attending to the nature of simple consciousness a philosophy of mind worth its salt will gradually reach a clear focus on more complex mental expressions such as choosing or deciding. Philosophical psychology shows us how the European mind has come to be what it is. The structured development of mind derives from the awareness of feelings. Consciousness comes about when we notice not only the sensuous experience of tasting the food, hearing the noise or smelling the odour, but also the emotions which accompany this noticing – the pleasure at the taste, say, or the fear at hearing the noise, or the repugnance at the odour. Feelings, such as pleasure and pain, are states to which we bring our attention. They do not constitute the attention itself. Further, our feelings are immediate since they exist only when they are sensed. As such, the realm occupied by our feelings is the realm of the given. What we are feeling at the time of the 'here and now' is given to us unexamined, unattended to, or, even, unidentified. To examine, attend to, or identify our feelings is to bring to bear on them more refined activities of consciousness. It is to reflect on the origin of the fear; to ask whether the fear is genuine or imagined, or to compare it with similar feelings experienced in different circumstances either in the present or in the past.

In *The New Leviathan* Collingwood denies that feelings have objects. It makes no sense to speak of a feeling like an ache as if it expresses a cognitive relation to its object. Feelings are not objects of observation which we attend to from the outside in, as it were. In this respect, Collingwood's account of feelings comes close to Gilbert Ryle's in *The Concept of Mind*, but there is a significant sense in which Collingwood parts company from Ryle. Since this raises a general difficulty in Collingwood's philosophy of mind it is worth mentioning here. Collingwood is insistent in speaking about the awareness of feelings as the first level of consciousness. Attending to feelings is, however, an activity of a different logical order. Collingwood may very well be right about this; but why *must* we think of simple awareness as the first stage of consciousness. Sometimes we know nothing more about a feeling than the experience of it; at other times, say, when we are jealous of someone, we have to know more if the feeling is not to be just a momentary or vague sense of resentment. In other words, the ways our different feelings operate are too diverse to fit the hierarchy that Collingwood plans for them.

To sustain the ordered picture of mind that is at issue here Collingwood must show how logical movement takes place between one level of consciousness and its successor. In becoming aware of our feelings Collingwood claims that we also recognize them for what they are, i.e. essentially ambiguous and indeterminate states that come when they come and, in Collingwood's own phrase, 'begin to perish as soon as they begin to exist' (*NL*, 5.5). Feelings are evanescent in ways both temporal and logical. They evade capture in the memory nor can they be expressed in terms of generalizations. No feeling is either single or multiple, part or whole. What enables us to find our feelings is language – only, Collingwood says, 'by talking about them, whether in speech or any other language' (*NL*, 6.22) do we become conscious of the feelings we have. The language of feeling, however, can only be an inventory of those feelings. It can be no more or less sophisticated than the feelings it expresses. What explains the development of consciousness from the level of feeling to its successor is not language alone – Collingwood argues that 'as consciousness develops, language develops with it' (*NL*, 6.58) – but a state which impels us beyond feeling without abolishing it. That state is, Collingwood claims, hunger, or, more generally, appetite. What appetite involves is the act of selective attention. It means abstracting or evoking from one set of feelings a different range of possibilities. Appetite is, therefore, the first move away from the condition of feeling per se. To reflect through appetite is to stand back from feelings and focus on how they can be responded to or dealt with. Appetite is a form of wanting, but one which leaves its object as yet indeterminate or unspecified. So Collingwood writes –

> Appetite is a name for the inherent restlessness of mind ...choice and reason and goal are not among the sources or conditions of appetite, they are among its products. (*NL*, 7.69)

The language Collingwood uses here reflects clearly his conception of philosophical method. So how does the method explain the full development of mind? What are the steps which link appetite with choice, reason and goal? Collingwood considers that appetite takes two forms – hunger and love. Hunger is an act of selective attention. As such it signifies the presence of abstract or conceptual thinking. Collingwood speaks of the ability to identify our feelings as the origin of conceptual language (a point I will explore further in the chapter on language). The development of consciousness through its different stages parallels the development of language. What hunger and love in different ways name are needs which seek for satisfaction. Hunger names a physical need. Love names our dissatisfaction with our solitariness; it is a necessary response to the frustration which arises from the self-centredness of appetite. Only by distinguishing between self and not-self can this frustration be calmed, since love necessarily transfers attention directly to the other. Echoing Hegel ('love, therefore, is the most tremendous contra-diction', *Philosophy of Right*, translated T. M. Knox, Addition 101, Paragraph 158), Collingwood finds that love, in promising an escape from the incompleteness and loneliness of the individual state, succeeds only in producing its own frustrations in the form of the passions – fear and anger. In love the individual becomes subject to the power of the other. Fear of loss and anger at absence are responses provoked in the lover by the recognition that the loved is autonomous, not totally in the control of the lover, not totally an object of play. It is the element of freedom necessary to love which distinguishes it from more primitive need satisfactions. With the arrival of fear and anger consciousness takes a further distinct logical step. Fear and anger are the only passions that Collingwood acknowledges. In both a concept is formed, not only of the individual's own state, as it is in appetite, but also of something else, namely the object which threatens or arouses. Fear is the response of cowering away, anger that of fighting back.

The importance of the passions in Collingwood's philosophy of mind is substantial. They form the link between conceptual and propositional thinking. Fear and anger come into existence only through reflecting on the objects which provoke them. In this way, the passions provide us with the experience of alternatives – of whether to yield or to fight back. Without this experience our appetitiveness would remain undirected and so would not produce the directedness of desire. Appetite is transformed into desire through the positing of alternatives. To desire something is not simply to want it; it is to know what is wanted and why. Desire involves an exclusiveness in picking out its objects which can come about only by interrogating them. In singling out the object we desire we commit ourselves to rejecting others. Why, then, should this process generate propositional thinking? It does so, in Collingwood's view, because the result of asking the question – 'what do I desire – this or that?' – is a statement of fact which can be either true or false. Identifying desires, as with all propositional thinking, is an activity in which it is possible to be mistaken, and with this possibility Collingwood's philosophy of mind moves to the edge of his thinking about ethics because it raises the nature of the human good, in other words, the difference between true and false desires, and what is worthy of being desired.

Ethics proper could not come into existence if mental development stopped with desire. In desiring we are impelled in one direction or another. We do not choose. Of course, desire requires alternatives, but in desiring we do not contemplate these freely. It is only by standing back from our desires and reflecting on them that we can be said to choose. Choice, therefore, exists in a distinct order of consciousness because it involves the possibility of thinking about our desires reflexively, for example, reflecting on our own happiness and setting it aside for some greater good. The exercise of choice is another way of describing the state of being free. To be liberated from choice is to possess the capacity of free choice. It is to be conscious of an equivalent capacity in others and, hence, lays the basis for the ethical notions of mutual self-respect and self-denial. Giving and understanding reasons for our choices are essential here because they make choice ethically determinate by opening it to moral scrutiny both from ourselves and others. Without an appropriate language, however, choice would be incapable of articulation. This gap Collingwood fills with the language of practical reason in which the reasons for acting one way rather than another are elucidated in a logical progression as criteria of rational action.

Before turning to a general discussion of Collingwood's philosophy of mind I would like to look briefly at two of its more unusual features. These are important because they play an interesting role in his account of presuppositions and also his aesthetics. The first concerns Collingwood's treatment of the unconscious. Given his scornful dismissal of psychology as a merely empirical science of mind it may come as a surprise to learn just how seriously Collingwood takes this notion. In spite of his express admiration for Freud – he refers to him as 'the greatest psychologist of our age' (*PA*, p. 64) – Collingwood does not analyse the unconscious exclusively in Freud's own terms. Indeed, it would have been impossible for Collingwood to do so given his view that what we know about our feelings can come only from our consciousness of them. On Collingwood's account there can be no such thing as unconscious feeling for the simple reason that we cannot experience feelings of which we are, at the same time, unaware. How, then, does Collingwood square this position with Freud? He attempts to do so, first, by re-interpreting 'unconscious' to mean 'pre-conscious' – so, it would be perfectly possible, Collingwood thinks, for someone to feel cold without noticing it. Such pre-conscious feelings are latent in the sense that they may become conscious. On this argument, we cannot have feelings of which we are unaware unless they are pre-conscious, but, then, we might ask Collingwood, how is it possible to describe them at all unless we become conscious of them?

Collingwood's second manoeuvre regarding the unconscious places him closer to Freud. What the unconscious refers to is the disowning which occurs when an experience is found so disturbing or repugnant that it is impossible to attend to it consciously. Collingwood concurs with Freud's identification of repression as signifying the process by which individuals reject those feelings they cannot consciously own. But, again, we might ask Collingwood, how is it possible to 'find' an experience disturbing without being conscious of it? Collingwood's difficulty here is compounded by his wanting to see the 'unconscious' and the 'pre-conscious' in terms of the levels of consciousness essential to his whole philosophy of mind.

The idea of the unconscious as the realm of the unfaceable, of that which must be disowned, is connected with the corruption of consciousness, the second provocative feature of Collingwood's philosophy of mind. Collingwood uses this term in both general and specific ways. In its general sense it refers to those forms of understanding, such as realism, which deform life through their false accounts of it. In its specific sense Collingwood uses it to refer to the denial or avoidance of feelings. It is, therefore, a special kind of insincerity because it involves both repression and frustration. When consciousness is corrupt the refusal to acknowledge feelings actually blocks the mind's development to a more complete and mature state. Corruption of consciousness is, for Collingwood, 'the worst disease of mind' (*PA*, p. 284) since it can permeate everything of significance that human beings do. How we are to assess Collingwood's proposals for preventing the disease or curing it when it is said to be in place depends in large measure on the persuasiveness of the tests Collingwood adduces for its presence. Here Collingwood's account is not without ambiguity either in relation to art or politics where the notion of corruption of consciousness is most commonly deployed. To raise simply two problems for Collingwood: is corruption of consciousness the result of deliberately misplaced attention or mistaken judgement? In addition, so as to overcome the corrupt state is it sufficient to own up to the feelings we have or must we also move beyond them to some more complete condition?

When we give general consideration to Collingwood's philosophy of mind a number of difficulties present themselves. The philosophy of mind involves many of the most intractable problems in philosophy, indeed, in its contemporary state some philosophers conclude that these just *are* insoluble. Certainly, Collingwood's way of proceeding is not likely to appeal to the supporters of physicalist or naturalist views of mind, but that, we might say, is no reason to dismiss him. Collingwood's difficulties stem primarily from the way he dissolves the mind/body problem. If mind and body refer not to two different things, but one thing understood in different ways then which of these ways offers the best explanation of mental life? Collingwood seems in one place (*The New Leviathan*) to defend philosophy, in another (*The Idea of History*) history – 'it is by historical thinking…that we discover the thought of a friend who writes us a letter, or a stranger who crosses the street' (*IH*, p. 219). This is, of course, a general problem in Collingwood's thought, one to which we will have good reason to return.

If, however, it is through philosophy that the mind is to be understood then Collingwood's account raises difficulties in terms of the evolutionary structure mind is said to possess. Collingwood takes great pains to stress that philosophy should not be too distant from the facts – 'the question is not about possibilities but about facts' (*NL*, 5.84) – but what if the facts about our mental life are too intricate to be encompassed in the levels of consciousness that compose Collingwood's account of mind? What if our feelings, for example, admit of a far greater grammatical complexity than can be incorporated without loss into Collingwood's picture of them?

We have throughout interpreted Collingwood's philosophy of mind as fundamentally anti-Cartesian. This seems to point it towards the idea of a public language as an indispensable frame of reference for mental states. There is a sense, however, in which Collingwood might not go far enough in this direction. He understands anger, for example, as a bridge between lower and higher levels of consciousness. Anger is an emotion intermediate between one state and another, but is this sufficient to tell us what anger means? Could it be possible, on Collingwood's account, to feel angry about anything? Could *anything* count as an object of anger? If our reply is that not anything could sensibly count then our attention is drawn from levels of consciousness towards those public contexts which give 'anger' expressions their meaning. The philosophy of mind, as Collingwood understands it, overlaps closely with the philosophy of language. To explore his anti-Cartesianism further it is to his views on the nature of language that we must now turn.

Chapter 4
LANGUAGE AND EXPRESSION

Collingwood is often thought to stand outside the mainstream of twentieth-century philosophy. For some this is a good reason to disregard him; for others, his ideas come as a breath of fresh air. Exactly why, and with what justification, Collingwood is deemed marginal may be considered by looking at his views on language.

In the analytical tradition, as embodied in the work of Frege, Russell and the early Wittgenstein, what a philosophy of language is expected to reveal is the correspondence between language and the world. The structure of language mirrors the world since a resemblance can be shown between the sentence and what the sentence pictures. Discover the logic of language, and the problems of epistemology, metaphysics and sometimes, even, of ethics can be thought to dissolve. What preoccupies philosophers of language in this tradition is the structure of language, which means that the problems of language are seen as the problems of syntax. From this semantic perspective little attention is given to the role of experience and understanding in the use of language. It is, however, precisely these features of language that interest Collingwood.

There is a further point. For the analytical tradition the essential task of a philosophy of language is that of analysing the expressions language contains and this means, in effect, propositional logic. But Collingwood rejects this view of language entirely because he dismisses its two central claims: one, that the proposition is the true vehicle of thought and, two, that the world can be made intelligible through the components of the sentence. In this way

Collingwood can be read as anticipating the later Wittgenstein turning his back on the logical atomism of his youth. Does Collingwood stand to realist theories of language as the Wittgenstein of the *Philosophical Investigations* stands to the *Tractatus*? In part, the answer must be yes since both reject the realist view that language is a representation of the world. The difference here is, of course, that Collingwood had never been a defender of realism; he had, therefore, no realist past to disown. For him, the realist claim that a correspondence exists between language and the world had always been an unargued assumption.

It is the depth of Collingwood's anti-realism which singles him out. In other words, what interests Collingwood is not how sentences and words connect with reality, but how the development of language is linked to the development of consciousness. Collingwood's focus here is clearly not that of analytical philosophy. The proposition is not the paradigm model of language use, but is rather a specialized form of intellectual language, one which finds its role in the way language develops. For Collingwood 'when consciousness becomes conceptual thought ... language develops abstract terms. When consciousness becomes propositional thought language develops the indicative sentence as the standard verbal form in which to state the proposition' (*NL*, 6.58, 6.59). The aim is to keep propositional logic firmly in its place, but even in its confined state Collingwood finds the proposition insufficiently dynamic to convey the interrogative character of knowing.

Collingwood's emphasis on the different forms of language – of feeling, of abstract terms, of thought – suggests parallels with the later Wittgenstein's notion of language games, but we should be careful not to overstate this. In Collingwood's view, the business of philosophy is not to *describe* language games to bring out their logical diversity, but to show how they are linked – one language use necessarily emerging from its predecessor. The danger in this exercise is readily apparent. Concentration on the development of language points Collingwood towards an examination of how language originates and this is another way of asking how language is learned. Language and consciousness, Collingwood tells us, evolve together, but what is it about the way consciousness develops which gives meaning to language at each stage of its development? Or, to put the question more specifically, what is it about feeling the cold which enables the cold to be named? Collingwood's answers to these questions involve his theory of naming, a theory that in *The New Leviathan* he derives in part from Hobbes, but prior to examining this we should look briefly at his general remarks on the nature of language in *The Principles of Art*.

Language, Collingwood asserts, 'is activity; it is expressing oneself, or speaking' (*PA*, p. 254). As an activity it can be understood in different ways. One way is to analyse language as the medium of thought. This is the project of the grammarian and the logician. Treated as grammar language is studied scientifically by dividing it into its component parts, analysing their relations and the rules which govern them. This division of language is not, however, something which is discovered by grammarians independently of the methods they employ. On the contrary, it is brought to language by precisely the form of analysis that grammarians use. For Collingwood, however, language as a living, vital activity will always escape the attempt to capture it in classification and division. 'Language', he writes, 'as it lives and grows no more consists of verbs, nouns, and so forth than animals as they live and grow consist of forehands, gammons, rump-steaks, and other joints' (*PA*, p. 257). As expressive of life's incon-sistencies, idiosyncracies and occasional arbitrarinesses language can never be totally within the grammarian's control. A perfectly consistent intellectual language must fail because inevitably it will be false to those anachro-nisms and contextual uncertainties which make ordinary life what it is. The grammarian, Collingwood writes, 'is a kind of butcher, converting (language) from organic tissue into marketable and edible joints' (*PA*, p. 257). Treated as logic 'the aim is to make language into a perfect vehicle for the expression of thought' (*PA*, p. 259). For Collingwood, both Aristotelian and modern analytic theories of logic when applied to language do not explain language but modify it after their own image. Words expressing emotions are to be replaced by statements analysed as propositions. Some logical theories propose that language conform to mathematics by using symbols instead of words. This 'intellectualization' of language, as Collingwood terms it (*PA*, p. 263), can never be total because then even a scientific language would disqualify itself as a language and become a mere terminology. In Collingwood's view, all language serves to express emotion; therefore, an intellectual language must either incorporate the appropriate emotions or destroy itself as a language.

Collingwood is resistant to grammar and logic as perspectives on language because he thinks that they hold ambitions beyond their means. To examine logical questions, say, the status of necessary truths, by understanding their role in our conceptual language is, Collingwood may be taken as saying, well within territorial limits, but to see language *as* logic will assuredly leave everything that makes language a human activity out of account.

So what does Collingwood mean by language? What kind of activity does he think it is? In *The New Leviathan* he refers to language as 'any system of bodily movements, not necessarily vocal, whereby (those) who make them *mean* or *signify* anything' (*NL*, 6.1). Since to speak is to mean something, language should not be confused with what happens to be its bodily vehicle. A vocal language, for example, does not consist in a system of sounds alone, but in sounds that signify something. A language of gesture does not consist in physical movements alone, say, the raising and lowering of an arm, but in movements that have meaning, say, to start the race, the beginning of physical exercise, or the attempt to recover from injury. As Collingwood understands it, therefore, language is not restricted to speech. A vocal language is one among a number of possible languages. Indeed, for Collingwood, speech itself is open to interpretation as a 'system of gestures' (*PA*, p. 243) each associated with a distinctive sound. What Collingwood wants to emphasize here is the mistake of linking language too closely to the expression of thought. As expression, language conveys meaning in a variety of ways – music, dance, facial or bodily gesture – and for many different purposes other than the intellectual.

The importance that Collingwood attaches to language is unqualified. Remove language and you remove what language expresses – whether it be a feeling, a concept or a thought. Language is the precondition of knowing, thinking and acting. While Collingwood is no behaviourist in his account of language – the starting of the race is more than the raising and lowering of the arm, the meaning of the thought is more than the complex physical operation required to express it – he argues, nevertheless, that language is indispensable to life. This is not because language represents how the world is or because it enables us to express our true essence. Language, in Collingwood's view, transmits neither facts nor essences, but expresses the development of consciousness in a unique way. Given this claim it is tempting to interpret Collingwood as telling us something about how our language – the predominantly scientific/intellectual language of the late twentieth century – has developed as it has. This temptation should be resisted, however. The language of thought does not displace that of feeling. Speech does not eradicate gesture. Precise definition does not eliminate pointing and gesturing, but, in complicated ways, arises from these, as a specialized language use does from a more basic precursor. 'If', Collingwood writes, 'a civilization loses all power of expression except through the voice, and then asserts that the voice is the best expressive medium, it is simply saying that it knows of nothing in itself that is worth expressing except what can be thus expressed' (*PA*, p. 246). In other words, for Collingwood, what language has the capacity to express is not simply a part of human life or a distinct mental faculty, but the whole person. Someone who uses language to the full, including gesture, speech, facial expression, etc., is able to express themselves, their feelings, emotions and thoughts with something approaching completeness. Defining, classifying and analysing are specialized usages which exhaust neither linguistic nor non-linguistic expression. In this way, Collingwood's account of language need not be read as confirming the development of a language which is largely intellectual in character.

Collingwood's claim that different civilizations display different uses of language has been taken as hinting at relativism. The suggestion that language is culturally variable may be understood to refer to the deviation in a particular way of life of gesture over speech. It may also refer to the ways linguistic conventions vary from one society to another, or depending on a given society's stage of historical development. What such cases present us with is the possibility that language use can be detached from language capacity. To those who have already set aside any commitment to language as a universal model of how the world must be, this possibility is not likely to cause much concern. For they will not see the history of language as culminating in the discourse of science nor will they see the survival of gesture as a form of communication necessarily prone to misunderstanding. However, what they will have to explain is how, within one set of linguistic under-standings, individuals can communicate with one another at all. Given Collingwood's view that linguistic under-standings are at one and the same time historical practices which can seek their validation only from within, such an explanation is one that we can reasonably ask from him.

It is to Collingwood's *The Principles of Art* that we should look for his answer. In learning a language individuals do not stand to each other as so many Robinson Crusoes, each wondering how their private definitions of terms so neatly coincide with those of everyone else. Language is essentially a communal activity. Collingwood links this point with the development of consciousness. Speech as a function of consciousness requires that there be speakers and hearers (Collingwood's terms, see *PA*, p. 247). All individuals have experience of these roles, even if only in speaking to themselves. Further, individual consciousness does not develop alone. In coming to an awareness of our own existence we are necessarily aware of the existence of others. We do not begin with an idea about ourselves which we then use by projection, inference or analogy to establish the existence of others. Rather, it is through the consciousness of the existence of others that we discover new sets of linguistic relations involving speakers and hearers other than ourselves.

When one individual communicates their fear to another this is not, Collingwood thinks, an experience like passing the parcel. It means bringing about something approaching the same state in that other. It means making that individual as fearful as you are yourself. Exactly how fearful is something that can only be expressed in language. Neither can stand outside language to compare their respective emotions. What is transferred is transferred in speech; what is received is received by being heard. But, further, both speaker and hearer are accustomed to articulating their own feelings to themselves and this experience provides, in Collingwood's view, the basis for their articulating their feelings to each other. Collingwood, however, says little by way of explaining this process. What exactly is it about self-articulation which enables mutual understanding? Collingwood's account of the relations between speakers and hearers leaves the answer unclear, even if we accept his main point that all language users are both speakers and hearers.

The gap in the argument here is not narrowed by Collingwood's statement that 'the community of language' (*PA*, p. 250) consists precisely in the relations between speakers and hearers as he understands them. It is this picture of speakers and hearers which lies behind Collingwood's claim that we do not first possess a language and then use it. Articulating our feelings to ourselves and others is not a use of language which comes after its possession, as practising a foreign language might follow from a grasp of the lexicon. To have a language of self-articulation *is* to use it and this is what a linguistic community consists in. But isn't this to run together two separate arguments? One concerns the relationship in language between possession and use. When Collingwood writes, 'one does not first acquire a language and then use it. To possess it and to use it are the same. We only come to possess it by repeatedly and progressively attempting to use it' (*PA*, p. 250), his words convince because they discourage us from thinking that there is one formula which can capture the diversity of language. This is the sense in which Collingwood can be read as anticipating Wittgenstein's view that 'to understand a language means to be master of a technique' (*PI*, p. 199). Collingwood's second argument, however, is altogether different. Self-articulation of feelings as a basis for mutual understanding represents just one way of using language. Collingwood makes a vital point when he says that we do not first have a language and then use it, but he wants to see one single use as paradigmatic for human communication. For Wittgenstein, using a language means grasping the rules which govern the many different expressions language contains. From this standpoint, what explains the linguistic community is not the interchangeability of speaker and hearer, but the rules to which individuals must subscribe in order to use language intelligibly. Here Collingwood's commitment to forging a link between language and consciousness seems to confine language rather than make its variety more transparent to us. His denial that the acquisition and use of language are two different activities is, however, clearly a move in a more Wittgensteinian direction because it is suggestive of how a language is learned.

In Collingwood's view, the acquisition of language is closely connected with the growth of consciousness. Feeling in its raw, physical state becomes an object of consciousness by being attended to. Attention cannot be explained in terms of introspection. 'Feeling cold' is not a description of a mental state or process, but an expression. We do not become conscious of such feelings by a kind of inner perception since this merely reproduces the original question in a different form and, hence, answers nothing. Something quite opposed to introspection is required, therefore, and Collingwood finds this in language. 'Feeling cold' is a linguistic extension of naturally expressive behaviour. Language and consciousness are two sides of the same coin since the identification of the feeling is a linguistic act. Language as expression is fundamental not only to the feelings, but also to more intellectual activities such as thinking, knowing and reasoning. The origin of language can be found in the human need to express, but why must this need be satisfied in language? For Collingwood, it is not possible to answer this question by considering language in its most developed form. He writes –

The grammatical and logical articulations of intellectualized language are no more fundamental to language as such than the articulations of bone and limb are fundamental to living tissue. Beneath all the elaboration of specialized organisms lies the primitive life of the cell; beneath all the machinery of word and sentence lies the primitive language of mere utterance, the controlled act in which we express our emotions. (*PA*, p. 236)

What Collingwood wishes to uncover here is the nature of language in its most elementary form. This cannot be achieved by rendering language as mathematics or logic, nor is it possible to discover what lies behind language. In *The Principles of Art* Collingwood draws a close connection between language and imagination – 'language is an imaginative activity whose function is to express emotion' (*PA*, p. 225). But this does not tackle the problem either because, as a definition, it does not address the character of language in its simplest form, as yet unmixed with intellect. Imagination arises, in Collingwood's view, only *after* the capacity to attend to feelings has developed and it presupposes a measure of self-awareness and, hence, freedom. The uncovering of 'the language of mere utterance' is an altogether more fundamental enquiry.

For Collingwood, consciousness of feelings means attending to them and this means expressing them in language, but, then, we must ask, what does this involve? What is the connection between, say, feeling the cold and expressing the feeling in speech? Collingwood's broad answer in *The New Leviathan* is that we become conscious of a feeling by naming it. The complex series of transitions which make up language originate in naming. Prior to this, feelings are pre-conscious since they have not been articulated. Awareness of naming a feeling moves the acquisition of language forward from naming to the grasp of abstract terms, to the understanding of concepts, the proposition and the language of practical reason.

Since naming is the load-bearing concept in Collingwood's account of language it is worth asking some questions about it. We become conscious of feelings by naming them. Collingwood asks what tells us that someone has noticed they are cold, and he answers –

He *names the feeling*. Perhaps he uses the language of speech and says 'cold'. Perhaps he uses the language of gesture and gives an expressive shiver. (*NL*, 6.25)

Now, what notion of naming is this? Is naming a paradigm of language, the first intelligible use or one use among many? Clearly, there are a number of difficult problems here. First, any sensible account of naming must acknowledge a difference between naming in a language already learned and naming in learning a language for the first time. Second, Collingwood's emphasis on naming might encourage us to think of language on the basis of the model of ostensive definition. Obviously, not all naming and certainly not all language use follows this model, which suggests that ostensive definition is not the sense that Collingwood is looking for. What, then, is Collingwood's view? In the case of naming in a learned language Collingwood accepts that naming, say, a previously unnoticed or unexperienced feeling is not like encountering an unrecorded mountain and giving it a name. Nor is it like coming across a plant, say, and trying to remember what its name is, but what Collingwood does not do is make the Wittgensteinian point that follows from this. Naming in a learned language is not a matter of attaching words to objects like so many privately bestowed prizes, but rather of grasping the conventions which govern the correct and incorrect use of the term.

A different set of difficulties emerge when we try to give an account of naming for the first time. How do very young children in learning a language come to name their feelings? Not, Collingwood believes, on the basis of having an object, say, a chair, pointed out to them and saying 'chair', since pointing is an activity in language and so cannot be used to explain it. If children already know what pointing means we want to know how because, as Collingwood rightly says, 'you can never teach a cat what you mean by pointing' (*PA*, p. 227). Naming, whether of objects or feelings, cannot be arrived at by pointing for the simple reason that pointing itself needs to be learned. Further, Collingwood argues, naming does not come from children listening to the babel of talk going on around them and discovering what stands out because this too presupposes an independent grasp of what it is to name something as opposed to general talk about it. In rejecting 'pointing to' and 'standing out' as explanations of how children first speak about their feelings Collingwood is, of course, at one with Wittgenstein. But in his own account Collingwood does not see language acquisition as a matter of learning the rules governing linguistic behaviour, nor, it must be said, does he see it as reflecting deep linguistic structures present in the way we are made. Collingwood's own answer is that children through repetition and growing physical and mental maturity convert the involuntary, expressive cries of hunger, cold or pain into deliberate utterances. The development of language, then, begins with children tumbling to the connection between the linguistic act and what it expresses. With the increasing awareness of oneself and others, linguistic differentiation also expands to express both more complex emotions and the orders of consciousness which succeed them.

Collingwood's essential difficulty in his philosophy of language is explaining the stages of language acquisition such that he can account for the transitions between them. Consider, for example, his claim that naming a feeling for the first time involves the conversion of an involuntary cry into a deliberate utterance. How can we make sense of one thing being converted into a very different thing? Surely, no amount of repetition of the cry will explain how it comes to be transformed into a name. Likewise, the child in learning that its cry names what it is feeling must also learn how to identify the same feeling when it occurs on different occasions. Learning how to express the feeling in a newly discovered linguistic form means learning how to extend it to new experiences. Thus, learning how to name the feeling involves learning the rules which govern naming in that language. It is not the act of naming that is basic, but the rules which give naming its sense.

Of course, Collingwood is not the only philosopher to run into difficulties in giving an account of language acquisition which relies on naming. What is notable about Collingwood, however, is how naming remains a significant feature of his theory of language in the later stages of consciousness. Collingwood speaks about how someone might be free from a particular desire; that individual will become free '*by naming it*; not giving it any name that comes at haphazard into his head, but giving it its right name, the name it really has in the language he really talks' (*NL*, 13.42). Whether naming the desire is a sufficient condition of liberation from it is clearly an open question, but surely what is not an issue is that naming a desire is not like naming a feeling for the first time. Naming a desire, especially in Collingwood's terminology, presupposes general familiarity with naming; naming a feeling for the first time does not.

One final remark about Collingwood's philosophy of language may be appropriate. Sometimes Collingwood refers to naming something in speech; at others, he refers to naming as a specific way of speaking. Nowhere does he think of names in the manner of the early Wittgenstein as component parts of propositions – 'An elementary proposition consists of names. It is a nexus, a concatenation of names' (*TLP*, 4.22) – but neither does he explore naming as one of the many different practices language contains. Collingwood has an explanation for both rejections. To discover what it is we must next turn to his views on logic.

Chapter 5
A REVOLUTION IN LOGIC

In logic Collingwood considered himself to be a revolutionary (*A*, p. 52). For most modern logicians, however, Collingwood's proposals are a storm in a teacup; they have not, therefore, been interested in giving its contents a vigorous stir. If Collingwood's contributions to logic are considered at all it is usually by writers on his intellectual history, but even these have tended to leave his logical discussions unconvinced. Three subjects dominate in Collingwood's thinking about logic – his criticism of propositional logic, the logic of question and answer and the logic of presuppositions.

The views Collingwood considered so revolutionary derive in large part from his double dissatisfaction with realist and idealistic logic. Realism ignores the ways in which our picture of the world depends on the questions we ask of it. Our knowledge of the world is composed only in part of assertions about it, so, for Collingwood, those 'acquainted with knowledge at first hand have always known that assertions are only answers to these questions' (*SM*, p. 77). But, equally, Collingwood is forced to accept the realists' main insight that for questioning to make any sense there must be something about which questions can be asked. Yet Collingwood's anti-realism does not throw him headlong into support for idealism – 'idealistic logic', Collingwood writes in his *Autobiography* (p. 52), 'was a confused mixture of truth and error. Mostly it was propositional logic; but in part it was a logic of question and answer.' In this respect, Collingwood sides with the later Wittgenstein in recognizing the inadequacy of propositional logic, but why does he think it fails? By what means does he replace it?

Understanding Collingwood's views on logic is very largely a matter of getting to grips with a comment he makes in *The New Leviathan*: 'it is a great work of folly to over-estimate the value of logic, or to think that anything can be done with it that cannot be done just as well without it' (*NL*, 45.31). Now, why, we want to ask, should Collingwood make such an apparently throw-away remark? In part, the answer is because he thinks that, in general, what matters to logic is not always what matters to philosophy. In part, again, it is because he denies that formal logic can capture his conception of philosophical method as employing a scale of forms. In part, also, it is because he rejects the possibility of a formal logic which is neutral as to the content of statements and inferences. Logic considers thought exclusively in terms of the abstract concepts which belong to logic and this means, for Collingwood, that it cannot describe 'thinking as it actually goes on' (*SM*, p. 273), but only 'the rules which thought, when it is valid, obeys' (*SM*, p. 273). If, additionally, logic is taken to *reflect* the structure of reality, then, Collingwood is at pains to point out, we succeed only in generating further illusions – that propositions can picture facts, for example, or that dialectic reveals unity in diversity.

Collingwood's revolution in logic, as he expounds it in *An Autobiography* and *An Essay on Metaphysics* (it is these texts that we must examine to discover what he says about the logic of question and answer and presuppositional logic), follows from his refusal to be beguiled either by realist or idealist logical doctrines. In fact, what lies behind both, in Collingwood's view, is a common dependence on the proposition as the true vehicle of thought, a dependence which wrecks their claims to be taken seriously as theories of logic and, also, of language. Collingwood's critique of propositional logic is notable, therefore, not simply for its brevity, but also for its anticipation of the ways the later Wittgenstein queries the *Tractatus* idea of the rules of logic telling us how to think or determining in advance how our understandings will go. In this respect, it is worth noting that in his *Autobiography* (published 1939) Collingwood tells us (*A*, p. 42) that he first developed his criticism of, and alternative to, propositional logic in 1917 (just four years before the publication of Wittgenstein's *Tractatus*), in a work (later partially destroyed) called *Truth and Contradiction.*

Collingwood takes issue with propositional logic on each of its central grounds. Propositions are not assertions, but answers to questions. In order to understand *what* is asserted it is necessary to discover the question which the assertion is meant to answer. This implies that question and answer are related correlatively – 'a highly detailed and particularized proposition must be the answer, not to a vague and generalized question, but to a question as detailed and particularized as itself' (*A*, p. 32). The correlativity requirement – that precise questions are necessary to produce precise answers – is not in itself a decisive challenge to propositional logic, but neither is it a complete account of the logic of questioning since it tells us nothing about which questions to ask beyond the rule that they must in some sense match the answers we are looking for. Collingwood's criticism of propositional logic takes a more radical turn in his application of the correlativity principle to the idea of contradiction. From this he concludes that two propositions are not inconsistent with one another *unless* they are answers to the same question. This seems to commit Collingwood to the view that no logical relations – whether of contradiction or implication – can exist between statements unless they belong to a question and answer framework. In Collingwood's alternative logic, logical relations hold only between questions and answers.

Collingwood has rightly been thought revolutionary in the way he puts contradiction to the sword, but he is even more so in his denial that truth and falsity belong to propositions as such. Truth and falsity are not properties of propositions, but attributes of question and answer complexes. In this theory, no answer is by itself true or false. It is right or wrong only in relation to the process of questioning of which it is a part. Further, Collingwood accuses propositional logic of assuming that truth-statements must take one propositional form, an assumption which, he claims, stems from the confusion of logic and grammar. Collingwood's rejection of the idea of logic/grammar interdependence is uncompromising and bears a close resemblance to the views of the later Wittgenstein. There is, however, a significant sense in which Collingwood, as a critic of propositional logic, stands alone. For Collingwood, but not for the later Wittgenstein, what replaces propositional logic is the logic of question and answer. Meaning, truth and falsehood, contradiction and agreement are not properties of propositions as such, but of question and answer complexes. What, then, does truth relate to if it is not the proposition? Collingwood answers –

> What is ordinarily meant when a proposition is called 'true', I thought was this: (a) the proposition belongs to a question and answer complex which as a whole is 'true' in the proper sense of the word; (b) within this complex it is an answer to a certain question; (c) the question is what we ordinarily call a sensible or intelligent question, not a silly one, or in my terminology it 'arises'; (d) the proposition is the 'right' answer to that question. (*A*, p. 38)

In developing his new logic Collingwood is not unambitious. Question and answer is taken as sweeping away all theories of truth in which the proposition is the central element. Propositions are not true or false simply in themselves, or because they correspond to some factual state of affairs, or because they do or do not cohere with other propositions, or because their truths reside in the expediency produced by believing them. All argumentation, as he expresses it in *The Idea of History*, 'depends on asking a question' (*IH*, p. 273). The terms of modern logic – assertion, judgement, inference – actually block our grasp of this, but, for Collingwood, the history of philosophy teaches us otherwise. Descartes, Bacon and Socrates are, in Collingwood's estimation, 'the three great masters of the Logic of Questioning' (*IH*, p. 273) – in this respect, he avers, 'so far as modern works on logic are concerned, Descartes might never have lived' (*IH*, p. 273).

What should we make of Collingwood's revolution in logic? The question is important because the first two stages of the revolution – the overthrowing of propositional logic and its replacement by the logic of question and answer – significantly influence Collingwood's philosophy of history, just as its third stage – presuppositional logic – shapes his metaphysics. Question and answer, as we shall discover, is vital not only to historical method, but also to the status of historical knowledge. For Collingwood, the truth of a proposition is inseparable from its function as an answer to a question, not any arbitrary question, but the real question to which it is the answer; this implies that the knowledge involved here is, in some strong sense, historical. Collingwood's new logic, then, is fundamental to his understanding of history and to his metaphysics, but what are we to make of it as logic?

Unsurprisingly, perhaps, defenders of propositional logic do not find Collingwood's challenge difficult to resist. They point out that propositional logic does not involve a necessary commitment to 'a one–one correspondence between propositions and indicative sentences' (*A*, pp. 35–6), as Collingwood charged. Propositional logic need not entail a defence of the idea of a logically perfect language. Collingwood's accusation that it does is an exaggeration typical of his later writing. They argue, further, that propositional logic can quite easily incorporate the ways that the contexts in which propositions are expressed can sometimes help to determine their meaning, and they reject Collingwood's claim that it is not possible to find a proposition true or false unless the question which it is meant to answer has been identified. Surely, they reply, some propositions can confidently be regarded as true in complete ignorance of their being answers to questions, even if that is what, in fact, they are.

When we move to Collingwood's account of what the logic of question and answer involves it is apparent just how easily defenders of propositional logic can turn defence into attack. Even if we allow, they will say, that every statement is an answer to a question (in what non-trivial sense can an exclamation, say, be an answer to a question?), how can we identify *which* question, out of any number of possible questions, the statement is intended to answer without an independent grasp of what the statement means? Collingwood's argument is circular – in order to know what the statement means we must understand the question, but this is not possible unless we know what the statement means. They will claim, further, that Collingwood plays fast and loose with the notion of truth. In denying that truth/falsity are properties of propositions Collingwood argues that only what he calls 'a question and answer complex' (*A*, p. 38) can be termed 'true', but if this is so it can be 'false', and, then, it becomes difficult to see in what sense it is 'false'. It is hard for Collingwood to sustain his position here without falling back on the propositional logic he claims to have overthrown. Such a concession may be inevitable given the problem of showing how the standard terms of propositional logic – truth, falsity, contra-diction – can be squeezed out of the logic of question and answer.

The counter-revolutionary assault on Collingwood's new logic can be pressed further. The view that no two propo-sitions are contradictory unless they are answers to the same question is intended to deny a basic principle of propo-sitional logic, but it does so only on the assumption that the logic of question and answer itself answers the same question as propositional logic, and this might not be the case. Collingwood, of course, makes precisely this assumption, which means that rescuing his revolution in logic is largely a matter of releasing him from it. Our initial thought must be that where Collingwood goes wrong is in thinking of the logic of question and answer as a *substitute* for propositional logic. Rather than constituting a revolution in logic as such, the logic of question and answer would then be seen as a fascinating method for throwing light on those kinds of thinking, in history, for example, which propositional logic cannot capture. We can then interpret Collingwood as saying that whereas propositional logic is appropriate to a specific kind of formal thought its overwhelming weakness is that it says little about thinking as a process of enquiry. The logic of question and answer is intended to fill this gap by showing that we think not in a series of mechanical movements from one proposition to another, but in a sequence of questions, each following the other in the right order. It is a matter of debate, of course, as to whether Collingwood does actually need a logic here as opposed to an account of method, or a hermeneutic, but what is clear is that to sustain the idea of thinking as the raising and answering of the right questions in the right order Collingwood has to provide a systematic account of how such questions suggest themselves. Without an explanation of this it would be hard to make *any* sense of his picture of truth as belonging to question and answer complexes. What, then, explains how questions arise?

At this point, it is worth reminding ourselves just how deep a dilemma Collingwood faces. In rejecting propositional logic Collingwood also rejects the ideas of truth and falsity associated with it. In asserting that which may be either true or false the proposition tells us something about the world, but what makes us convinced that asking questions in the right order – the answer to one question necessarily giving rise to the next – will achieve the same result? Collingwood has to show that questions do not arise arbitrarily, but out of rational necessity. In other words, he has to show that questions do not emerge from an intellectual void, that there is some rational basis for the questioning process taking the course that it does, and that we have good grounds for regarding at least some answers as final.

For Collingwood, the solution to these problems is to be found in the logic of presuppositions. With this stage explained, Collingwood's revolution in logic is concluded, although, as we shall discover, not necessarily secured. In Collingwood's view, every statement in systematic thought is an answer to a question. Every question arises only on the basis of a particular presupposition. Thus, my statement, 'I have not stopped attending meetings of the Philosophy Society', derives its meaning not in isolation, but in response to the question, 'Have you stopped attending meetings of the Philosophy Society?'. This question, in turn, cannot arise unless it is presupposed that there exists a Philosophy Society whose meetings I have attended in the past. Questions, answers and presuppositions stand in specific logical relations to each other. They make up a series in which the answer to one question becomes the presupposition of the next. Understanding the question which a given statement is meant to answer involves uncovering the presupposition in whose absence the question could not have arisen. However, no series of questions and answers can be infinitely long. So Collingwood postulates the existence of a special kind of presupposition which is not an answer to a question, but what kind of presupposition could this be?

In Collingwood's theory a given set of presuppositions must be present for specific questions to be meaningful. Such presuppositions are either relative or absolute. Both give rise to questions, have what Collingwood calls 'logical efficacy' (*EM*, p. 28), and are subject to change. But while relative presuppositions make questioning possible *and* are themselves subject to it, absolute presuppositions are concerned solely with its possibility. It is because relative presuppositions can be answers to questions that they are verifiable, i.e. shown to be either true or false. Absolute presuppositions, on the other hand, can never be answers to questions, and, therefore, they are not propositions. From this it follows that as truth/falsity can be predicated only of propositions absolute presuppositions are unverifiable. Collingwood does not mean that we want to verify them but are unable to, but that their logical force is not dependent on verification; it is dependent only on their being supposed. Relative presuppositions are subject to the normal process of question and answer in a way in which the absolute kind are not. It is not that absolute presuppositions are ultimate questions or unanswerable questions. They are not questions at all. Any attempt to treat an absolute presupposition as if it were relative is meaningless, as Collingwood remarks:

> ... any question involving the presupposition that an absolute presupposition is a proposition such as the questions 'Is it true?'; 'What evidence is there for it?'; 'How can it be demonstrated?', 'What right have we to presuppose it if it can't?', is a nonsense question. (*EM*, p. 33)

To illustrate this point Collingwood asks us to consider three distinct modes of scientific enquiry – the Newtonian, the Kantian and the Einsteinian. Each involves a peculiar notion of causation in the absence of which they could not be made intelligible. And in each their notion of causation operates as an absolute presupposition of their scientific practice. It is not that it is true or that they think of it as true, but that they simply take it for granted.

Such absolute presuppositions do not occur in isolation, but are found in interlocking systems which Collingwood calls 'constellations' (*EM*, p. 66). In an interesting contrast with Wittgenstein it is worthy of note that Collingwood does not think of these as language-games, at least not as modelled on the idea of 'the tools in a toolbox' (*PI*, p. 11). Collingwood writes:

> The constellation, complex though it is, is still a single fact. The different presuppositions composing it are all made at once, in one and the same piece of thinking. They are not like a set of carpenter's tools, of which the carpenter uses one at a time; they are like a suit of clothes, of which every part is worn simultaneously with all the rest. This is to say that, since they are all suppositions, each must be *consupponible* with all the others; that is, it must be logically possible for a person who supposes any one of them to suppose concurrently all the rest. (*EM*, p. 66)

We might describe 'constellations' as a priori conceptual schemes which establish the background of certainty necessary for the process of question and answer to take place. This background of concepts cannot itself be made subject to truth/falsity because it is what enables us to distinguish between truth and falsity at all. Such a conceptual scheme operates, therefore, as a determinant of meaning, of what, in any particular mode of discourse at any specific historical time, will count as an intelligible question. In taking this for granted we acknowledge its certainty and, thereby, provide a limit to scepticism.

There is a great deal in these ideas which brings Collingwood very close to the later Wittgenstein, particularly in *On Certainty*, where he writes, 'the *questions* that we raise and our *doubts* depend on the fact that some propositions are exempt from doubt, are as it were like hinges on which those turn' (*OC*, p. 341). Both Collingwood and Wittgenstein make the point that it is not that we try to verify the conceptual background and are frustrated when we discover that we are unable to do so, but rather that the question of its verification cannot arise. While Wittgenstein does not speak of absolute presuppositions he insists that the conceptual background is not dependent for its existence on individual choice. Wittgenstein writes, 'But I did not get my picture of the world by satisfying myself of its correctness; nor do I have it because I am satisfied of its correctness. No: it is the inherited background against which I distinguish between true and false' (*OC*, p. 94). Collingwood remarks, 'We do not acquire absolute presuppositions by arguing; on the contrary, unless we have them already arguing is impossible to us' (*EM*, p. 173). We should not, however, press Collingwood's affinities with the later Wittgenstein too far. One crucial difference between them concerns the cognitive status of those deep-lying conceptual structures in which absolute presuppositions play a fundamental part. Collingwood never completely concedes to the view that such structures need nothing outside themselves to fulfill their cognitive role. Wittgenstein, however, regards the 'form of life' (*PI*, p. 19) as logically ultimate. There is nothing beyond the language we use. We have reached the limits of what can be sensibly expressed.

Collingwood, albeit with great difficulty, develops his theory of absolute presuppositions on a very different basis because he wants to show how absolute presuppositions change. The history of a scientific practice, for example, reveals that the deep conceptual structures which govern the raising and answering of questions within the practice are themselves subject to change. How is this possible if there is no way, independently of those structures, of arguing with them or disproving them? Wittgenstein's solution is in the form of an analogy – 'And the bank of that river consists partly of hard rock, subject to no alteration or only to an imperceptible one, partly of sand, which now in one place now in another gets washed away, or deposited' (*OC*, p. 99), but Collingwood seeks a less metaphorical account of this process. He is concerned with how changes in the 'hard rock' take place, with what strain, however imperceptible, it is subjected to. Quite obviously, any theory of how absolute presuppositions change has to be consistent with their nature. For Collingwood, the logical efficacy of absolute presuppositions depends only on their being supposed. It is meaningless to try to demonstrate their truth/falsity. Our standard methods of achieving knowledge by doubting what is established, asking questions the answers to which provoke new questions, are, therefore, precluded. We cannot ask for evidence or proof of either a logical or an empirical kind since absolute presuppositions determine what we can and cannot ask. On Collingwood's own account, therefore, absolute presuppositions do not change by reference to conventional canons of rational enquiry, but change they do and in his *Essay on Metaphysics* he tries to explain how they do.

Note, first, however, what kind of explanation Collingwood cannot give. Absolute presuppositions cannot change by reference to criteria of rationality outside themselves since this would countenance precisely the realist insight that Collingwood wishes to disclaim. On the other hand, Collingwood is clearly reluctant to allow that conceptual structures can be judge and jury in their own case or that we can construct *any* set of hypotheses with which to square the verdict of experience. His solution (if such it is) is to say (and this is really the only thing he can say) that absolute presuppositions change from within. Any given 'constellation' of absolute presuppositions will contain strains which test the permanence of the whole structure. When these are kept in check each absolute presupposition in the structure is 'consupponible' (*EM*, p. 66) with the rest. So, Collingwood writes:

> ... the absolute presuppositions of any society, at any given phase of its history, form a structure which is subject to 'strains' of a greater or less intensity, which are

'taken up' in various ways, but never annihilated. If the strains are too great, the structure collapses and is replaced by another, which will be the modification of the old with the destructive strain removed; a modification not consciously devised but created by a process of unconscious thought. (*EM*, p. 48)

The use of inverted commas and the dependence on metaphor in this passage reveals Collingwood's failure to solve the philosophical problem he sets himself. The use of the expression 'unconscious thought' equally gives the game away. For Collingwood to have made absolute presuppositions *subject* to rational interrogation would have been to make them indistinguishable from relative presuppositions. On the other hand, to have divorced them totally from that scrutiny would have been to banish them to a logical vacuum. To explain their change in terms of unconscious thought, however, seems to deprive absolute presuppositions of their character as thought. How can absolute presuppositions act as the yardstick of rational questioning if they have no rational basis themselves?

The problematic status of absolute presuppositions forces us to ask by what form of enquiry we can know what they are. Collingwood's answer is clear. The science which detects the absolute presuppositions of intellectual and practical life is metaphysics. Human enterprises exist in time and their continuity depends on the transmission of absolute presuppositions over time. Absolute presuppositions are, therefore, matters of historical knowledge and this brings metaphysics into close conjunction with history, a conjunction for which, as we shall see in a later chapter, Collingwood has to provide a persuasive defence. Collingwood's revolution in logic has brought his thinking into treacherous philosophical waters. What began as an attack on formal logic has, through a series of not altogether convincing transformations, ended with the apparent conversion of metaphysics into history. To prepare for the discussions to come we next examine Collingwood's philosophy of history.

Chapter 6
THE HISTORICAL IMAGINATION

If there is one area of philosophy on which Collingwood's reputation as a philosopher is based then it is surely the philosophy of history. Similarly, if one of Collingwood's works ranks above all others in terms of public discussion then it is surely *The Idea of History*. Generations of readers have received their introduction to Collingwood through his philosophy of history without necessarily knowing very much else about his thought. What they discover is that his ideas regarding the possibility, nature and value of historical knowledge are provocative and, indeed, unavoidable for anyone approaching the philosophy of history for the first time. Of course, Collingwood's philosophy of history has its own history. His views do not come to us, any more than they came to him, neatly packaged. His reflections on history, as his *Autobiography* makes clear, were hard-fought, and, in this respect, their development reveals considerable shifts in position and modification to respond to new influences, like Croce, or to take on new intellectual targets, such as Spengler, about whom Collingwood writes, he 'lacks the true historical mind' (*EPH*, p. 67). But what, in Collingwood's view, is 'the true historical mind'? To answer this question it is necessary to distil the essential features of Collingwood's philosophy of history, but we must, first, as is almost always the case with understanding Collingwood, examine the accounts of history he rejects.

Collingwood is in no doubt about the form of thought which makes history most opaque to us. By adopting science as its explanatory model, realism is, Collingwood believes, completely blind to what makes history possible. The realist wants to say that there exists a world of facts independent of concepts and categories. Science pictures this world as a kind of repository of data held together by laws or law-like generalizations. History, however, cannot proceed on this assumption since what the historian aims to understand is the past, and the past no longer exists. It is remote from us, dead to human observation. If the past is another country it is one we can never revisit. So, on the realist account, history is either modelled on science, in which case it is a travesty, or it has no logical basis. Collingwood, of course, argues otherwise. For him 'the chief business of twentieth century philosophy is to reckon with twentieth century history' (*A*, p. 79).

History, then, cannot be ascertained as fact, but how can it be understood? Collingwood's answer reflects two remarkable features of his philosophy of history. He answers, first, as a philosopher who wishes to explain what is distinctive about history as a category of thought. In this respect, Collingwood wants to show what makes history possible, not simply as a way of saying something about the past, but as saying something that is true. He answers, second, as a practising historian of Roman Britain who approaches the problem of historical knowledge with a trained historian's eye. As philosopher and historian Collingwood does not believe that historical knowledge can be confined to the activities of historians. It is far too important for that. Historical knowledge concerns how individuals and societies have come to be what they are. It is not restricted to the remote past – to the exploits of Alexander or the sack of Rome – but informs our contemporary sense of who we are. For Collingwood, it is through historical thinking 'that we discover the thought of a friend who writes us a letter or a stranger who crosses the street' (*IH*, p. 219).

In Collingwood's view, historical knowledge becomes more like a condition of human understanding than an explanation of the past, although, as we shall discover, the contrast between present and past implied here is never, for Collingwood, so sharp or clear-cut. What human beings share when they share a language or a thought is something that is grasped through their capacity to reconstruct each other's purposes. Historical thinking tells us as much about how we understand each other as it does about how we understand the past. Collingwood sees these under-standings as intimately connected with the refutation of scepticism, as, indeed, does Wittgenstein: 'If experience is the ground of our certainty, then naturally it is past experience. And it isn't for example just *my* experience, but other people's, that I get knowledge from' (OC, p. 275).

But how *can* history play such an essential role in our lives if the past no longer exists? Not, Collingwood argues, through the common-sense or what he calls the 'scissors-and-paste' (*A*, p. 115) view of history. To confine knowledge of the past to testimony in the form of recorded observa-tions, as the common-sense view effectively does, is to accept a realist model of explanation, on the basis of which historical propositions assert on grounds of testimony that an event occurred at a specific time. History consists in accepting or denying such assertions, but, of course, as Collingwood very well knew from his own experience as an historian, history would not be history at all if historians merely duplicated their sources. Through imagination, interpolation and criticism historians must range far beyond the authorities they use. In the common-sense view, histo-rians have no licence to contradict authorities, nor to give one priority over another. But, Collingwood insists, if there is no logical basis for such questioning, the common-sense view must be false since it is only through questioning that history lives.

How can historians question the past when the past no longer exists? Only, Collingwood argues, if the past is not dead, but in some way living in the present. What makes history possible is that past and present do not exist in a state of permanent separation, but overlap one with the other, the past remaining in the present in the shape of evidence. So Collingwood writes – 'if there were a past event which had left no trace of any kind in the present world, it would be a past event for which there was no evidence and…no historian…could know anything about it' (*A*, p. 96). Historians uncover past events by considering the evidence – in the form, say, of weapons, pottery, diaries, etc. – but what kind of consideration is this if it does not employ the methods of natural science? In treating artefacts as evidence historians are, in fact, asking questions rather than simply making assertions. Historical knowledge consists in drawing inferences from what the evidence indicates as having happened. The appropriate model here is not the physicist but the detective interrogating evidence to reconstruct a past sequence of events. History comes to life as the interpretation of evidence, but, Collingwood now asks, what makes the drawing of inferences possible? What entitles us to think of inferences as valid?

The history with which Collingwood is concerned is, of course, human history. Likewise, the artefacts the historian examines are human artefacts, but what enables the historian to understand them as such? Unearthing the sword tells us nothing about the motives of the individual who raised it; uncovering the beaker says nothing about the state of mind of the person who drank from it; reading the diary may give no information about why it was kept. And, yet, it is precisely these considerations that make such finds significant. Understanding human artefacts, therefore, whether in the past or the present, is, in Collingwood's view, a matter of grasping the ideas which give artefacts their life. In this respect, historical understanding in general is much closer to the way we understand ideas than it is to our understanding of natural processes. In *The Idea of History* Collingwood puts this point in a way many critics have found misleading – 'the historian, investigating any event in the past, makes a distinction between what may be called the outside and the inside of an event' (*IH*, p. 213). By the 'outside' Collingwood refers to the physical movements of individuals, say, an army crossing a plain; by the 'inside' he means the ideas which give the movements their human point – what is the army doing? Is it being forced into a retreat, mounting an invasion, or engaged in a military exercise? However, what is clear is that Collingwood does not regard the thought as operating like the ghost in the machine. As we have seen when discussing his philosophy of mind Collingwood is no Cartesian. His point here is a straightforward one. The historian's business is with human actions, not solely with events. Further, actions and events exist in different logical categories since the former can be understood only in terms of the thoughts of the agents who perform them. This means that, for Collingwood, 'all history is the history of thought' (*A*, p. 110), but, then, on what conditions can a past thought be understood? First, the thought must be expressed, either in language or in a non-linguistic form of expression, and, second, the thought must be capable of being rethought by the historian who is trying to understand it.

In stating these conditions Collingwood should not be taken as making history so intellectual that it fails to encompass life. The thoughts that historians grasp embrace many human purposes in addition to the strictly intellectual. A theorem in early Greek geometry, the practice of entomology in ancient China, an abdication crisis, a medieval Welsh love spoon or a nineteenth-century Cornish dance – all are open to historical explanation. But what form does this explanation take? The historical past is studied inferentially on the basis of evidence. Inferences are possible because the historian is able to reclaim past thought. In so doing history ranges far beyond the acceptance of testimony, but, Collingwood insists, a plausible account of the past requires something more than inference. We can point to this in the following way. An historian knows, for example, 'that one day Caesar was in Rome and on a later day was in Gaul', but 'nothing about his journey from one place to the other' (*IH*, p. 240). According to Collingwood, what fills this gap in the narrative is an act of interpolation. To interpolate is to move from what is known to what can be reasonably believed. So, far from indicating a degree of historical failure interpolation is fundamental to history because it shows clearly that the historian's task is that of *reconstructing* the past. In bridging narrative gaps the historian need not be thought arbitrary or fanciful. Interpolation must be at least consistent with the evidence. For Collingwood, the presence of interpolation in historical thinking tells us something crucially important. To interpolate is to imagine, and imagining, say, Caesar travelling from Rome to Gaul, is, in Collingwood's view, indispensable to history. The historian understands the past by means of imaginary reconstruction, but the past can be reconstructed only on its own terms. Historical claims are truth claims and, as such, are subject to challenge by appeal to evidence. Imagination in history, therefore, is substantially different from imagination in art. In history imagination is disciplined by what the evidence allows the historian to say. Not anything can be imagined about the past since to avoid anachronism the past has at least to be understood in its own setting.

By stressing the role of imagination in history Collingwood is not making history unreal or fictitious. It is not the act of imagining which creates the unreality, but *what* is imagined. H. G. Wells imagined men on the moon. A modern historian can do the same, but with evidence to support it. The picture of the past that the historian imagines must be consistent with the evidence, but, further, it must be coherent in the sense of giving us an intelligible narrative. Collingwood's understanding of the nature of historical knowledge is, perhaps, best found in the following passage:

The historian's picture of his subject, whether that subject be a sequence of events or a past state of things, thus appears as a web of imaginative construction stretched between certain fixed points provided by the statements of his authorities; and if these points are frequent enough and the threads spun from each to the next are constructed with due care, always by the *a priori* imagination and never by merely arbitrary fancy, the whole picture is constantly verified by appeal to these data, and runs little risk of losing touch with the reality it represents. (*IH*, p. 242)

In our account of Collingwood's philosophy of history we have so far concentrated on what makes history possible, but history also claims to show why the past takes the form that it does, and we need to understand how this can be. Here our focus must be less to do with how we can understand what happened, but rather *why* it happened. According to Collingwood, what gives history its licence to truth in this regard does not come from natural science. In the realist view of history, asking for an explanation for the occurrence of something means asking what caused it. For the realist, the question 'why did x occur?' is equivalent to 'what caused x?'; but, for Collingwood, this is precisely not how history proceeds. Since history is not concerned with events but actions, it cannot explain actions in terms of causes. To offer an historical explanation of action is to look for the agent's intention or motive in performing it, and this, in Collingwood's language, is another way of saying that the historian must rethink the thought in the agent's mind. But how does this explain why the action was performed? Here we encounter one of Collingwood's boldest doctrines. He writes:

For history, the object to be discovered is not the mere event, but the thought expressed in it. To discover that thought is already to understand it. (*IH*, p. 214)

In other words, the historian in grasping that something has happened knows simultaneously why it happened. Historical understanding takes the form of re-enactment. Re-enacting the thought of another means putting yourself in their place so that the world is seen from their point of view. In achieving this the historian discovers the projects that individuals set for themselves and how they follow them through. For Collingwood, the capacity to rethink the thought of another is a condition of history. Without it the words of a Napoleon or a Nelson would be to the present empty of meaning. However, re-enactment creates a problem. If the historian understands Napoleon's thought by rethinking it then there is an important sense in which we have not one thought, but two – Napoleon's thought and Napoleon's thought as re-enacted by the historian. What, Collingwood asks, is the difference? It is one of context. To Napoleon the thoughts of exile he experienced on Elba were present thoughts. To the historian rethinking them they are thoughts encapsulated in the historian's present. In rethinking Napoleon's loneliness, therefore, the historian cannot feel loneliness as Napoleon felt it. The past lives in the present not as experience, but as self-knowledge. In Collingwood's view, historical thinking does not preclude criticism of the thought it re-enacts. Re-enactment:

> ...is not a passive surrender to the spell of another's mind; it is a labour of active and therefore critical thinking .... It is an indispensable condition of the historical knowledge itself. (*IH*, p. 215)

It is the link between history and self-knowledge which provides the clue to history's value. Through historical thinking individuals and societies come to know who they are and what they might accomplish in the future. Past and present do not live separate conceptual lives, but overlap one with the other. In this overlap, the past does not stand to the present as alien, but, through re-enactment, lives on in it. If valid, therefore, Collingwood's philosophy of history marks the refutation of solipsism as much as it does historical scepticism. But that 'if' has loomed large in the minds of Collingwood's critics, so we must test it to see if its use is justified.

Objections to Collingwood's philosophy of history have been made by historians as well as philosophers. It is worth pointing out, however, that Collingwood's arguments relate to the conceptual status of history. They concern the possibility of history as a distinct form of understanding. What he says about the historical imagination, for example, is conceptual rather than empirical in character. With this in mind, it is noticeable, nevertheless, that none of Collingwood's central theses have escaped critical attention. Let us debate these in turn.

Consider Collingwood's thesis that all history is the history of thought. Surely, the objection might run, history is not about thought, but facts. Historians are not interested in what was thought to be the case, but what was the case. In minimizing the role of factual assertions in history Collingwood makes it more corrigible than it need be. Indeed, he has been read as making it impossible for natural events to be included in history at all. But these objections do not address Collingwood's main point. There is an essential difference, Collingwood argues, between explaining natural processes and understanding human conduct. Human conduct involves concepts which are internal to it. No history of human conduct can proceed, therefore, without an acknowledgement of this. Further, anyone who thinks of human history *as a repository of fact* ignores this difference and, since past facts are, as facts, inaccessible to us, is unable to explain how history is possible at all. Likewise, natural events are important to the historian only insofar as they enter human consciousness. It is not the date alone that matters, but what the date signifies – a birthday, a declaration of war, or an act of assassination.

For Collingwood, the historian understands a past thought by re-enacting it, but this gives rise to further questions. First, is what the historian re-enacts restricted to past thought? And, second, is it through re-enacting the thought that the historian understands it? In the first criticism Collingwood's doctrine stands accused of limiting history. Only rational reflection can be reconstructed, but that seems to exclude actions which are impulsive, compelled or 'thoughtless' and to ignore these is to make human history a somewhat bloodless affair. Collingwood's best response to this would appear to be to widen the notion of thought beyond rational reflection. If by thought Collingwood means consciousness then what is excluded from history becomes more defensible. From this stand-point, the historian could not re-enact the unconscious, or the immediacy of human feelings. Napoleon's urge to build an empire could not, then, be explained in terms, say, of repression. What he thought about his feelings in exile would be open to re-enactment, but not what his feelings as he experienced them meant to him. Is it through re-enactment, however, that the historian works? It may be the case that in thinking historically we recapture a past thought, but, then, what is recaptured is not unaffected by the methods used to recapture it. The original thought, say, the piety of St Francis of Assisi, did not involve those methods, nor does re-enacting the thought enable the historian to think of himself as St Francis did.

A criticism of a slightly different kind, but a horse from the same stable, nevertheless, is that in construing history as the history of past thought Collingwood converts history into biography. Critics following this line will point out that not all thought takes the form of individual thinking. A human practice, say, the American Constitution, involves thought, but this is not reducible without loss either to its original formulations or the subsequent individual contributions to it. Similarly, human history includes some thought which, at a high level of abstraction, defines an age.

Medieval Christianity, the revival of learning, or the Enlightenment are, in some sense, conceptual schemes which are intelligible independently of their individual components. There seems, however, no reason why Collingwood need be troubled by this objection. Indeed, the idea of history as the history of past thought, linked in Collingwood's hands with the doctrine of absolute presuppositions, provides a fruitful basis for thinking about those general conceptual frameworks which give a way of life its distinctive character. Such vocabularies are spoken by individuals, but they are not the invention of a single individual. Since the absolute presuppositions of a society are not open to doubt they may operate as Kuhnian paradigms which ground questioning without being subject to it. Collingwood's philosophy of history not only embraces this possibility, but is highly suggestive about how the texture of such broad structures of thought is to be studied.

Perhaps the doctrine in Collingwood's philosophy of history which has given his critics most difficulty is the claim that when historians understand what happened they also know why. The re-enactment of the past thought tells us all we need to know about the agents involved and the circumstances that face them. This seems, however, to fly in the face of common sense. Even in purely intellectual cases which seem to best exemplify it, Collingwood's view is unconvincing. The historian of chess, for example, can understand the thoughts in Spassky's mind in the 1972 contest with Fischer without necessarily grasping why he failed to win it. In practical life Collingwood's position seems even less tenable. An historian knows that in 1940 Hitler failed to invade England, but this knowledge does not entail knowing why. Collingwood's idealism is here at odds with the realist recognition that the historian must be concerned as much with the situation that faces historical individuals as with their thinking about it. It is true, of course, that success or failure in history *can* be traced back to the state of mind of the individual concerned, most notably, perhaps, in cases involving weakness of will, but this is not always so. Whether or not striving is successful most commonly depends on the situation, independently of what anyone thinks about it. This means that Collingwood's view here leaves much of the historian's work unexplained.

Collingwood's critics have often cast a sceptical eye over his stress on imagination in history, arguing that this undermines the notion of historical truth by making it too dependent on the historian's subjective, possibly idiosyncratic, picture of the past. However, Collingwood's defence against this charge seems secure. It is not the act of imagination itself which produces the fiction, but what is imagined. There is an important difference between my imagining my garden devoid of trees and my imagining fairies at the bottom of it. Nothing in Collingwood's doctrine requires him to think of history as more like the latter than the former. Collingwood certainly thinks of the historical imagination filling gaps in the narratives *and* guiding the reconstruction of them. If he is, at times, unclear about the differences between these two exercises this does not weaken his basic defence.

Collingwood's philosophy of history departs significantly from romanticism because he does not think of history as an art form, but he does, nevertheless, give the historical imagination a crucial role. In this respect, imagination counters that form of scientific arrogance which deems the practices of societies remote in time to be inadequate approximations of our own. Imagination is primarily a term of art. To discover what Collingwood means by it in that context we must raise the subject of his aesthetics.

Chapter 7
THE LIFE OF ART

In any consideration of Collingwood's aesthetics the main focus must be on *The Principles of Art* because it is here that we find the mature expression of his aesthetic theory. Collingwood's text is not, however, solely concerned with the nature of art and art criticism. The work ranges widely to include questions concerning literary criticism, cultural value and the relation between art and the community. More importantly, *The Principles of Art* is as much a primary source of Collingwood's philosophy of mind as it is of art, and it contains, too, the essence of his understanding of language, especially in its association with art. In terms of its subject matter, therefore, *The Principles of Art* is not an uncomplicated text. For philosophers interested in aesthetics, however, Collingwood is important because of what he says about art – what it is and why it should be taken seriously. Attending to Collingwood means responding to his arguments; indeed, dismantling Collingwood's arguments is often thought of as a kind of basic training in aesthetics. From this point of view, *The Principles of Art* is not a systematic treatise on the interconnections between mind, art and language, but the source of a theory of art which is simply mistaken.

Such a critical stance need not disregard the origins of Collingwood's aesthetics, nor the main influences on it. Plato, Coleridge and Hegel among historic figures, and Croce, Alexander and Carritt among Collingwood's contemporaries all play a considerable part in shaping his own thinking, but if a single philosopher stands out as pivotal then, surely, it is Vico. It cannot be an accident that

Collingwood's first book was a translation of Croce's *The Philosophy of Giambattista Vico*, published in 1913. From Vico, to some extent mediated by Croce, Collingwood gleaned a number of important insights into the nature of art which his own aesthetics attempts to deepen and clarify. In Vico's original perception, art is, in some strong sense, closely connected with the feelings; identifying art involves showing how it is linked distinctively to the imagination; the character of art is bound up with the human need for expression, and the mode of expression which has most relevance to art is language.

All these doctrines figure strongly in the development of Collingwood's views on art as he formulates them in *Speculum Mentis* (1924), and *Outlines of a Philosophy of Art* (1925), but their most decisive expression is at the heart of his mature aesthetics in *The Principles of Art* (1938). What drew Collingwood to Vico may have been his own experience of an artistic education. Art in Collingwood family life was not thought of as a spectator sport. To enjoy it, Collingwood was taught by precept and example, it was necessary to engage in it. Collingwood was a not inconsiderable musician, so when he writes about art he writes from the standpoint of one who knows what it means to create something – a piece of music, say, or a drawing or a poem. Knowledge in art is inseparable from creativity, a principle which Vico took, in effect, as fundamental to all human activity. Collingwood derived much the same point from another important influence on his aesthetics, one he found much closer to home. Collingwood's father, W. G. Collingwood, was a landscape artist of note and a writer on art, especially the place of art in education and in the development of the critical faculties both in the individual and in the community. In any attempt to gauge the influence of father on son the crucial text is W. G. Collingwood's *The Art Teaching of John Ruskin* (1891). This work contains striking affinities with Collingwood's later aesthetics and its influence runs alongside Ruskin's own, often to the point where the two are difficult to disentangle. When Collingwood, in *The Principles of Art*, writes that aesthetic activity 'is a corporate activity belonging not to any one human being but to a community' (*PA*, p. 324) we hear a powerful echo of those Ruskinian ideas with which he had been familiar since youth. The distinction between art and pseudo-art, the close connection between art and the community, the intimate relation between art and the imagination – all such doctrines are at work in Ruskin's influence on Collingwood's formative thinking.

Ruskin could not, however, answer the philosophical question posed by art. In *Speculum Mentis*, Collingwood puts this question in the form of a paradox – 'the paradox of art is that it is both intuitive (pure imagination) and expressive (revelatory of truth)' (*SM*, p. 87). Art presents philosophy with a problem to be solved, but in his search for a solution Collingwood found little help from aesthetic theory. Neither Hegel nor Croce, the latter considered by Collingwood to be an especially ingenious thinker about the nature of art, gave him a satisfactory way of removing the contradiction. How can it be that art is *both* unconstrained imagination and revelatory of truths about the world?

Collingwood's first attempt to tackle this question is laden with difficulties. Art, in *Speculum Mentis*, is seen exclusively in terms of the idealist philosophy of mind which informs that work's grandiose structure. As the lowest form of experience art is defined as pure imagination, distinguished by Collingwood from both sensation and assertion. Imagination, unlike sensation, is active and has in beauty its own criterion of value. While works of art are neither true nor false, art unavoidably is suggestive of truth because it is expressive. Art is, therefore, internally inconsistent, and so finds itself superseded by forms of experience possessing greater coherence. In this account, the contradiction inherent in art is removed by requiring art to yield to cognitive thought. That this manoeuvre involves a downgrading of art should be plain, but, in any case, it makes sense only on the basis of the idealist picture of mind and its activities. Drop this picture and Collingwood's method for dissolving the paradox of art must surely vanish with it.

In *Speculum Mentis* the importance of art is as a stage in human development. However, thinking about art in this way does not effectively explain how art can be imaginative as well as expressive. In *The Principles of Art* it is this problem that Collingwood addresses through a sophisticated version of expressivism. For Collingwood, the purpose of art is the discovery of feeling and this is achieved through expression. It is, in other words, a condition of art that there are emotions which require expression and that a capacity of some kind exists to express them. Thus, towards the close of *The Principles of Art*, Collingwood tells us succinctly what he considers art to be –

> The aesthetic experience, or artistic activity, is the experience of expressing one's emotions; and that which expresses them is the total imaginative activity called indifferently language or art. This is art proper. (*PA*, p. 275)

Collingwood's conclusion that art is i) imaginative, ii) expressive, and iii) not just analogous with, but identical to, language is well-known. Also familiar is the close connection he draws in *The Principles of Art* between art and mind. Art and language are identical since each is expressive – art expressing the imaginary object in the mind of the artist, language the thought in the speaker's mind. Further, all acts of consciousness involve language. Thus, since art and language are alike all acts of consciousness must be imaginative. Language is expressive of different orders of consciousness. Every new linguistic utterance is, therefore, imaginative and may be considered art. The interconnections between art, language and mind could hardly be drawn any tighter than they are in Collingwood's theory. Here our focus will be on Collingwood's expressivism as an account of art. What is the essence of his view? What weaknesses does it involve?

The first point to notice about Collingwood's expressivism is how distant it is from the common-sense version. What matters to art, naïve expressivists claim, is emotion – both in the feelings of the artist and the emotional impact of the work of art on its audience. For the naïve expressivist, art expresses *and* produces emotional states. Novelists, say, express their feelings in literature. Readers respond through the emotional impressions novels have on them. Now Collingwood rejects naïve expressivism almost as completely as he does the common-sense 'scissors and paste' account of history. According to Collingwood, the naïve expressivist gives an oversimple explanation of the relationship between art and emotion. To say that art arouses emotion is to suggest an instrumental relationship. Art is the means; the emotion aroused, the end. But, Collingwood argues, a means/end vocabulary is characteristic not of art, but of craft. Art proper, as Collingwood terms it, must be distinguished from art as amusement and art as magic. Art is not a technique for the production of given effects in the form either of enjoyment or practical therapy. To think of art as craft is to allow that the emotion art arouses might well be produced in some other way, and this is to miss entirely what is distinctive about art. Additionally, a work of art may fail in the production of particular effects and still be judged good art – a further indication to Collingwood that it is necessary to draw a sharp distinction between art and the contingent effects which follow from it.

Naïve expressivism, in Collingwood's view, is also mistaken in thinking that the emotion somehow exists prior to the work of art which expresses it. The artist first experiences the emotion and then translates it into the work. On the contrary, in Collingwood's account, the experience and the working on it are inseparable. The feeling and the poem, say, which expresses it are inextricably linked – the one 'is conditional upon the other' (*PA*, p. 304). Here Collingwood is not saying simply that we can identify the feeling *only* in the poem, but, also, and more audaciously, that feeling a certain emotion is bound up with the artistic effort to express it. This points us to the crucial concept in Collingwood's own theory. Emotion is not expressed in the work of art in its raw, felt state, but mediated by the imagination of the artist. Through the exercise of the imagination, artists give concrete and articulate expression to the feelings which animate and provoke them. Creativity in art is not simply a matter of transferring the feelings to the canvas, the score or the page, but is rather a process of self-exploration and discovery in which the work of art is less a description of the original feeling than a manifestation of it in a newly articulated form.

In Collingwood's sophisticated expressivism imagination and expression play central roles. Art is a process of transformation in which artists do not follow predetermined guidelines, but struggle to give public shape to the clarity of vision which exists in their own minds. In this account of the nature of art Collingwood finds a powerful sign of its value. Since, as he puts it, 'every utterance and every gesture that each of us makes is a work of art' (*PA*, p. 285), art cannot be a luxury. Thus, for Collingwood, 'to know ourselves is the foundation of all life that develops beyond the merely psychical level of experience' (*PA*, p. 284), but in his aesthetics Collingwood lays greatest stress on imagination. The real artistic effort goes on in the mind of the artist. In relation to this the actual work of art seems secondary. What Collingwood emphasizes is what is going on in the artist's mind rather than on the canvas, the page or the score. The artist as craftsman makes his products according to a plan, one which is embodied in the finished product, as an engineer's drawing of the bridge is embodied in the bridge itself. However, this is not true of the artist proper whose activities are not concerned with bringing about specific ends. When a composer composes a piece of music, therefore, where is the work of art located – in the tune as the composer imagines it, the tune as actually performed or in the tune's notation on the musicians' scores? For Collingwood, the answer is plain –

> ... the music, the work of art, is not the collection of noises, it is the tune in the composer's head. The noises made by the performers, and heard by the audience, are not the music at all; they are only means by which the audience, if they listen intelligently (not otherwise), can reconstruct for themselves the imaginary tune that existed in the composer's head. (*PA*, p. 139)

In other words, for the tune to exist it is not necessary for the composer to sing it, play it or even write it down. These are only the accessories of art. The making of the tune goes on in the artist's head and nowhere else. Now, if this is the case with music it should apply with equal force to pictorial and literary art. As art proper a piece of music is no more something audible than a painting is a representation of something external. But, Collingwood claims additionally, both the music and the painting 'exist solely' (*PA*, p. 151) in the musician's or the painter's head. In making this claim he is clearly entering deep philosophical water for the simple reason that the 'tune in the composer's head' view of art is demonstrably false. If art proper is understood as a mental idea in the Cartesian sense then it seems wholly vulnerable to the full force of the Wittgensteinian assault. Are we really to believe that Bach, for example, stands as a privileged spectator to the tune in his head, viewing his genius from a privileged standpoint accessible only to himself? It seems hard to imagine a more unconvincing account of art. Further, Collingwood's critics point out, the 'tune in the head' theory of art seriously neglects the role played by the material the artist works with. The skills involved in moulding the clay or mixing the paint and applying it to the canvas are real, material skills. They do not exist solely in the artist's mind and, arguably, they play as important a part in the creation of the work of art as the artist's idea of it.

Now the easiest way of rescuing Collingwood from such deep philosophical waters is to show that he never actually enters them. Indeed, it would have been ironic if Collingwood, after rejecting naïve expressivism in favour of a more sophisticated version, found himself defending the equally naïve 'tune in the head' view. The simplest explanation, therefore, seems also the best. Collingwood does not support this view, at least not in the form suggested by its critics. We have seen already that Collingwood's philosophy of mind is not easily hoist with a Cartesian petard, and it is difficult to imagine a philosopher of art more familiar than Collingwood with the way artists actually work. Collingwood writes, 'a man paints with his hands, not with his eyes…what one paints is what can be painted…and what can be painted must stand in some relation to the muscular activity of painting it' (*PA*, p. 145). So what is Collingwood talking about? We can bring out his point in the following way. Understanding a work of art involves more than experiencing its external manifestation. Listening to a symphony with appreciation is not simply a matter of hearing a collection of sounds. Attending to a painting by Turner, for example, is not simply a matter of observing the arrangement of the figures or the use of colour. For Collingwood – and this is the important point he wishes to make – understanding a work of art is not the passive reception of what is given, but an activity of informed engagement in which the artist's original intuition is recreated. In listening to the symphony, therefore, we reconstruct or enter into the thought of the composer. In reading the poem we grasp the poet's original idea. We re-produce in ourselves the emotion the work of art expresses.

It is worth emphasizing that there is nothing in this account which requires Collingwood to deny that a work of art is essentially a public object or that it is only through what the artist has achieved that an aesthetic response is possible. Further, Collingwood's stress on the audience's collaboration in the realization of art is valuable because it makes explicit ways of noticing and listening in art which many readers will find familiar. Understanding a poem, for example, is often not complete on first reading. It is a process which grows as readers immerse themselves more thoroughly in what is being said. However, there is a difficulty here. Collingwood cannot assume that all readers will respond to the poem in exactly the same way. Different readers might agree that Yeats's *Easter 1916*, for example, is a fine poem because it possesses a certain grandeur of language, but they may differ completely over the emotions it is supposed to express. Now which reader has fully reconstructed the thought in Yeats's mind? To say that this question is answerable in terms of one response rather than another is to suggest that Yeats's thought can be grasped independently of reading the poem, but this Collingwood resolutely refuses to allow. Responding to Yeats's thought by drawing on material outside the poem which expresses it is to read Yeats biographically and this is to miss what is distinctive about his art. There are good reasons for thinking that this difficulty is not confined to literature. In music, for example, considerable differences exist between performances of the same piece of music. Leaving aside deafness or musical incompetence, this can be because performers interpret the score differently, but it may also be because they differ over the emotions the music is supposed to express. But, then, how is it possible to reconcile this difference when there is no way of estab-lishing what the composer's feeling is except by performing the music? The problem arises from Collingwood's expressivism. Does he have a solution to it?

Collingwood is aware that the idea of art as expression can be interpreted in a highly individualistic way. We have seen how diversity of response creates a problem, but there is a deeper issue. For Collingwood, the expression of emotion can be of value only to the individual whose emotion it is. Does this mean that the work of art is valuable only to the artist whose feelings it expresses? Collingwood denies this. He writes –

> the artist's business is to express emotions; and the only emotions he can express are those which he feels, namely his own ... he undertakes his artistic labour not as a personal effort on his own private behalf, but as a public labour on behalf of the community to which he belongs. Whatever statement of emotion he utters is prefaced by the implicit rubric, not 'I feel', but 'we feel'. (*PA*, pp. 314–15)

Art, as we have seen, is transformative. When art gives distinctive shape to the feelings it articulates it is expressing feelings that are shared. The self-knowledge that art discovers is not, therefore, in any sense esoteric. On the contrary, it belongs, in principle, to the community, which means that art, as Collingwood puts it, 'is the community's medicine for the worst disease of mind, the corruption of consciousness' (*PA*, p. 336).

This gives Collingwood a problem, however, one which may be called the artist's version of 'physician, heal thyself', for art can only provide a cure if it is first capable of removing the disease from itself. What, then, is a corrupt consciousness in art? Collingwood does not think that the difference between good and bad art is one of technique. Rather it is the difference between a truthful awareness of emotions and one that is corrupt. Bad art derives from corruption of consciousness, but how can this be? The answer is found in Collingwood's expressivism. Art is the expression of emotion, but not all emotions are expressed truthfully. In these cases, the artist falsifies the emotion by disowning it, repressing it or pretending that it is otherwise than it is. Failure of expression constitutes the difference between bad art and 'art falsely so called' (*PA*, p. 282) since in the latter there is no attempt at expression at all. Bad art falsifies the feelings by presenting them in a counterfeit way. By making something sentimental out of feelings that are perfectly natural, or by bowdlerizing emotions that are manifestly and unavoidably part of life, bad art not only falsifies itself, but is also false to life. Bad art just does not ring true. Good art is uniquely suited to the expression of the feeling that provokes it. Collingwood accepts that corruption of consciousness in art can never be total. Artists who present their feelings as otherwise than they are must know *what* they are transforming in order to do so. Just as those who are self-deceived must know a part of the truth about themselves, so insincere artists must be at least conscious of the genuine feelings they plan to fake.

In emphasizing the way sham art trades off the genuine article Collingwood is surely right because it is this fact that provides the basis for discrimination in art. In Collingwood's theory, however, discrimination is bound up with the emotional response of the discriminator and there are a number of occasions in his account of this where his audacity appears to get the better of his logic. The artist's business is with the expression of emotion, but why is the expression of emotion something to be valued? The value of art is that it brings our emotions to consciousness in a unique way, but this assumes that the artist's audience shares the emotions the work expresses. What does this involve? For Collingwood

...if art is the activity of expressing emotions, the reader is an artist as well as the writer. There is no distinction of kind between artist and audience ... the poet is not singular either in his having that emotion or in his power of expressing it; he is singular in his ability to take the initiative in expressing what all feel, and all can express. (*PA*, p. 119)

There is, however, a logical difference between the real and the fictional. Not everyone might weep at the death of Little Nell, some may not feel anguish at the blinding of Lear, but these are at least *possible* emotional reactions. Responding to the death of, say, Winnie Verloc in Conrad's *The Secret Agent* is, however, quite unlike responding to the death of a close friend. There is something wrong, in other words, with a reader who becomes too directly involved in the feelings the novel expresses. Being moved by a novel is very different from being moved by a situation in life. Collingwood is, of course, keen to deny that a response to a work of art can be a purely intellectual matter. Equally, he insists that art has no interest in the *direct* arousal of emotion, but in dispensing with any 'distinction in kind' between art and its audience he seems to give art a status in life it cannot possibly sustain.

One of the ways we show that art is important to us is by having discussions about good and bad art. Does Collingwood's expressivism tell us anything about what constitutes good art? The main point to note is that for Collingwood expressiveness is a necessary condition of art. This identifies art proper. Bad art falsifies the emotions by expressing them in a counterfeit way, but it is, at the very least, expression. Good art expresses the emotions in a way that is true to them; a way, in other words, that communicates exactly what they are. This seems to imply that the test of quality in art is largely negative. Good art is seen as art proper plus the truth condition. A work of literature that is directly concerned with arousing a specific emotional state in the reader is, therefore, not simply bad art, it is not art at all. We have seen how wide-ranging Collingwood's conception of art is. If art is expression then every expressive human utterance is an aesthetic utterance – 'every utterance and every gesture that each one of us makes is a work of art' (*PA*, p. 285) – but this seems of little help in deciding what is to count as artistic worth. Indeed, Collingwood's list of artists who pass the test contains few, if any, outside the expected canon – Dante, T. S. Eliot, Mozart, for example; a reflection, possibly, on the fact that Collingwood says little that is informative about what makes expressive art (there can be no other kind) good art.

Collingwood's lack of attention to questions of artistic worth derives from his expressivism. The question of whether a work of art is good or not (or even a work of art at all) is not answered by looking exclusively at psychological facts about the artist's mental processes. There is, further, all the difference in the world between an ordinary expressive utterance, a piece of abuse at a football match, say, and the expression of the emotions in Greek tragic drama. Sophocles's *Antigone*, for example, has an enduring claim on us, but how can expressivism account for this? It is of the essence of art, Collingwood tells us, that it is destructive of stereotypes. Art sweeps away illusions and, in this sense, all great art is prophetic. Collingwood writes –

The artist must prophesy not in the sense that he foretells things to come, but in the sense that he tells his audience, at the risk of their displeasure, the secrets of their own hearts. (*PA*, p. 336)

Art, in expressing the artist's feelings truthfully, destroys the pleasures produced by faked emotions. If the community is deceived then art is its therapy. Since, however, *all* human communities comfort themselves with illusions, the need for art is never lost. It is for this reason that great art lasts. This is, of course, a desperate and unconsoling picture as

Collingwood surely intends it to be, but notice how radically Collingwood's belief in art as therapy alters his expressivist conception of art. If art is therapy (albeit not of a crude psycho-analytical kind) then Collingwood must provide some way of showing that it has worked. But isn't this to admit that art has an end other than the imaginative expression of emotion at which it aims, and isn't this to convert art into a craft? Further, if art is therapy it would seem to follow that the artist does not merely contemplate the world, but actively attempts to change it. Collingwood certainly writes in this manner – 'art is not contemplation, it is action' (*PA*, p. 332). This suggests, however, that art is closer to politics than the art/craft distinction can allow. To explore this implication we must turn to Collingwood's view on action.

Chapter 8
CIVILITY AND CIVILIZATION

Collingwood's reflections on practical life are extensive, covering economics in addition to morality, politics and the nature of civilization. Rather than being a late interest prompted by political developments prior to the Second World War, ethical and political questions occupied Collingwood throughout his philosophical life. In *An Autobiography* (*A*, p. 147) Collingwood describes his attempt to discover a 'rapprochement' between theory and practice as having played a major role in determining his philosophical direction, and, in this respect, his autobiographical judgement is clearly right. We know from his earliest work in philosophy that, in opposition to the realist view that individuals occupy a world of facts to which thought makes no difference, Collingwood argued that thought is not peripheral to action but indispensable to it.

Speculum Mentis, Collingwood's first major work in the post-war period, is very much a call to order, an attempt to restate the unity of the mind to those 'wrecks and fragments' (*SM*, p. 36) who had survived the War. In *Speculum Mentis*, a philosophy of practical life parallels the philosophy of spirit, each form of mental experience making itself manifest in an appropriate form of action, the logic of the whole purporting to reveal that with the maturing of consciousness comes the attainment of freedom. Of course, Collingwood's thinking about action between *Speculum Mentis* and *The New Leviathan* (his major work in political philosophy) exhibits considerable change and development, but there is a strong sense in which *The New Leviathan*, too, can be considered a call to order since in its arguments mind, action and association are not examined as separate categories, but as interlinked; as Collingwood writes, 'civilization is a thing of the mind and a community too is a thing of the mind' (*NL*, 1.21). It is worth emphasizing that Collingwood's stress on the unity of thought and action is as much a feature of his liberalism as it is of his anti-realism. So when Collingwood writes about practical life he does so from the standpoint of the philosophical liberal for whom a philosophy of mind is a necessary preface to a philosophy of action. For Collingwood, the principle at the heart of liberalism is that of rational freedom. The philosophy of mind explains how human consciousness develops to the point where it becomes capable of reflective choice. With choice enters the possibility of rational freedom and, since all freedom is social freedom, choice is also accompanied by the associative life and the modes of practical reasoning appropriate to it.

Liberalism, as Collingwood understands it, involves the idea of rational freedom, the identification of political activity with political education, the primacy of dialectic as a method of achieving political agreement, and the claim that the acknowledgement of authority is not equivalent to being subject to the exercise of power. In a command theory of political obligation, obedience is reduced to submission and freedom travestied to mean compliance with external threat. For Collingwood, authority is not reducible to force, and freedom, rather than vanishing in the act of obedience, is a presupposition of it –

> only a free agent can obey; only one who is conscious of himself as a source of independent political energy can recognize that energy in another, and co-operate with it. Giving commands to anyone who is not intelligently free is as useless as making faces at a blind man. (*EPP*, p. 103)

A liberal society is characterized by politics construed as a distinct mode of conduct. Rejecting the idea that the state can be understood in terms of substance and attribute, Collingwood is concerned with politics as intelligible activity. In this respect, politics is distinguishable both from economics which looks to utility as its standard of judgement, and from morality because, as Collingwood puts it, 'a society makes a law not because it is its duty, but for some other reason – a political reason' (*EPP*, p. 95). Politics, economics and morality are not composed of actions as separate facts, but are distinct forms of experience according to which actions are understood. Political action, on Collingwood's account, is 'essentially regulation, control, the imposition of order and regularity upon things' (*EPP*, p. 100). Where there is political life, 'there is rule; both immanent rule and transient rule' (*NL*, 28.11). Politics as the creation of order incorporates the levels of practical reason insofar as these constitute different reasons for the making and enforcing of rules. Thus, political action contains will, as rule by decree; utility, as policy; regularian (Collingwood's term) action, as law; and duty, as the historical manifestation of concrete choices.

Since what Collingwood says about ethics and politics is shaped by his liberalism it is this which must be our centre of attention. Contemporary liberal philosophy is much preoccupied with how a liberal society which does not seek to impose a single view of human wellbeing can govern in accordance with principles of justice that do not presuppose any substantive conception of the good. Those who criticize this project on the grounds that its ethical premises are actually diluted in terms of any serious ethical content and that its central methodology completely ignores the moral density of character and circumstance are, in fact, echoing Collingwood's stress on self-understanding as a necessary feature of personal and social identity, and on historical knowledge as a necessary constituent of the way we think about ourselves and others. The contemporary nature of Collingwood's philosophy of history has often been recognized, but can his liberalism stand up to similar scrutiny? The first difficulty here is that Collingwood says nothing directly about justice, the concept which, in contemporary liberalism, is often seen as the first virtue of political and social institutions. The second difficulty is that it is abundantly clear that Collingwood does need such a concept, for without it his liberalism would lack an agreed criterion for evaluating the mutual relations of individuals within a political community, their relations with the world of nature or with other human beings not members of the same community. The third difficulty is that Collingwood's candidate for this conceptual role – civility – cannot be derived by appeal to utility or contract, for, in Collingwood's political phenomenology, the principle of utility construes disagreements as conflicts of interest and, hence, cannot explain how such disagreements can be subsumed under rules or ideals of civility. Equally, the idea of contract fails to explain how a political life embraces those who are in the process of learning its vocabulary, including its language of civility.

To what extent, then, can Collingwood's understanding of civility give liberalism the moral shape which its critics claim it lacks? Civility may be taken to refer to the practices of good government, the virtues of a citizen or those rules of conduct necessary for a decent social order. Collingwood does not share Nietzsche's view that civility is merely a mask for timidity, a socially convenient form of hypocrisy. For Collingwood, it is an ethical ideal which, as he puts it, takes its reference point from 'the ideal condition into which whoever is trying to civilize a community is trying to bring it' (*NL*, 34.7). In *The New Leviathan*, Collingwood is concerned with civility in a formal sense. To treat another with civility,

> means respecting his feelings: abstaining from shocking him, annoying him, frightening him, or (briefly) arousing

in him any poison or desire which might diminish his self-respect. (*NL*, 35.41)

In this minimal sense the language of civility is one of abstention; it is a virtue of forbearance or restraint, moderation and discipline, a virtue satisfied by *not* doing that which may be offensive, disrespectful or intimidatory. Civility can refer to the ways we respond to moral demands which are independent of it. It does make a difference, for example, as to exactly *how* rights are waived or asserted – with respect for the feelings of others, or with indifference and scorn. To emphasize civility as a way of morally attending to others is not, however, to construe it as a foundational virtue necessarily underlying all sense of value.

How, then, does civility stand in relation to politics? The question arises not from the conceptually 'thin' nature of civility, but from the need to show how it has a place in Collingwood's dialectical account of political action. It is tempting to answer this question by stressing the close connection between civility and politics as a developed form of experience. The process of learning to become civilized is at one with learning to become a member of a political society. In other words, the closer politics approximates to the full structure of practical reason the nearer it is to the ideal of civility. But is the relation between civility, civilization and politics quite so tight? One way of approaching this question is to unpack the formal and substantive characteristics of Collingwood's notion of civility to discover how they bear on his concept of the political.

Civility understood as an ideal to which all civilizations can only approximate relates to politics, first, in the sense that both presuppose a social existence, practical reason and a rational consciousness; and, second, in the sense that no political society is ever internally coherent and no political society can ever completely embody civility – in

Collingwood's view, 'the community's condition never becomes one of pure civility and the barbarous elements never vanish' (*NL*, 34.55). Collingwood acknowledges that even if civility is one ideal, 'there may be many approximations to that ideal, differing among themselves as shots on a target may differ not only as being at different distances from the centre but as distant from it in different directions' (*NL*, 34.66). So is there a civility appropriate to politics, to morality or to art? Or is civility an ideal state to which politics even in its most complete form must continue to aspire? The scale of forms analysis which Collingwood employs at many points in his thought is not obviously applicable here. The idea that concepts are logically related, not as genus and species, but as overlapping, hierarchically arranged forms cannot accommodate substantial collision between the demands of civility and the realization of non-reducible political goods. Further, analysis of moral thinking on the lines laid down by the scale of forms – utility, right, duty – is notoriously difficult to match against the actual and varied judgements made by individual moral agents. So even if civility and politics share common presuppositions this does not allow us to conclude that there are no significant disjunctions between them.

Civility bears further on politics in Collingwood's thought through the notion of respect. Civility is 'respect for others as shown in demeanour towards them' (*NL*, 37.15). To treat someone civilly, Collingwood writes, 'is an entirely different thing from an affectionate or expansive emotion, what is called "liking" him or "being fond of" him' (*NL*, 35.72). Such feelings may be consistent with the use of both necessary and unnecessary force, 'even though the object is in fact human and therefore according to the ideal of civility, entitled to civil treatment' (*NL*, 35.76). Clearly, Collingwood is attempting to protect civility against intrusion from likes, feelings and desires, but can this be achieved without diminishing its formal claims? Uncivil behaviour which is disrespectful but falls short of the use of force, such as scorn, indifference or contempt, can only be described substantially, that is, by revealing the content of the moral concepts concerned. Further, as Collingwood himself notes, there will be circumstances in which civility may have to be suspended or it may involve exceptions or exclusion clauses. Arguments regarding these, such as disputes over the treatment of strangers, are morally substantial and, therefore, pull the notion of civility closer to cultural definition and, hence, to political disagreement and debate.

In Collingwood's view, the rules of civility necessary to a society are transmitted not simply as rules of grammar or as rules of conversation within which individual inventiveness takes place, but in the full recognition that as a framework of conduct civility can be usurped by managerial or utilitarian needs or threatened by brutishness, interest, mere enthusiasm and vulgarity. Individuals in circumstances where civility is impoverished may find a source of renewal in the inner life – 'if you can look deeply enough into yourselves, you will find there… the means of living well in a disordered world' (*EPP*, p. 174) – but how does this leave the status of civility as an *ideal*? How does civility manifest itself politically as an *ideal*?

Collingwood does not interpret the logic of an ideal as an abstract principle which exists in utopian isolation from ordinary life. For an ideal to have a bearing on our world it must be in some sense present in it, perhaps, immanent in it, awaiting gradual realization. In *The New Leviathan*, Collingwood describes civility and barbarism as ideal states, but no actual society 'is just *civil*; no society is just *barbarous*' (*NL*, 34.52). Of course, the more advanced the process of civilization the closer it approximates to the ideal, although it can never reach this point completely. Collingwood clarifies his understanding of ideals in an important manuscript, 'What "Civilization" Means', which he wrote in late 1939/early 1940, in other words, around the time he began work on *The New Leviathan*. In this work Collingwood is at pains to distinguish his position from the relativist view that standards of civilized life are not universal, but derive from the form of life of any given society at a given period in its history. He writes – 'this is called "historical relativism", and is rightly regarded with suspicion, because…it amounts to denying that there is any such thing as an ideal of civilized conduct' (*NL*, p. 489). What the historical relativist ignores is the possibility of 'an ideal of universal civility; civility on every kind of occasion, civility under any kind of provocation, civility to every kind of person' (*NL*, p. 494). This order of ideal is associated by Collingwood explicitly with the Sermon on the Mount. Conditional rules of civility, being civil to particular individuals in particular circumstances, rest on 'the ideal of civility as such' (*NL*, p. 494). Collingwood writes –

This is the sense, and the only sense, in which all civilizations, or ways of living in a civilized manner, are one. They are one in the sense that they all converge upon this one ideal. It must be one ideal, there can be no other beyond it, because it is absolutely unqualified. There can be no fourth order ideal of civilized conduct between man and man. Every man must recognize it when he reflects on his own way of life as a member of a civilized society. He finds himself behaving civilly in certain limited ways. On reflection he discovers that he is trying to behave civilly in other and more far-reaching but still limited ways. On further reflection he discovers that he is trying to try to behave civilly without any limit whatever. (*NL*, pp. 494–5)

How do these orders of ideal fit with Collingwood's understanding of politics? The first order of ideal tells us how the principles of civility actually guide conduct, but not how they generate new limitations and permissions. The third order of ideal has no actual instantiation in life and serves as a method of assessing how far a society lives up to its own conditional standards. The second order of ideal is rooted in existence, but at the same time offers a criterion which judges what has been realized by reference to what remains unrealized. How does Collingwood construe politics in relation to civility conceived in this way?

Civilization is an activity of mind. As with all human conduct it is an approximation to an ideal state. Civilization means learning to follow the rules of civility. It means refraining from diminishing another's self-respect by recognizing their freedom of choice and refraining from the unconditional use of force over them. In Collingwood's view, it is the impossibility of *complete* civility which gives politics its point. No civilization can ever totally remove those elements of savagery which always remain within it as 'primitive survivals' (*NL*, 9.5). Further, in any civilization civility will be threatened by barbarism – the deliberate attempt to put the civilizing process into reverse. Politics finds its primary role in converting non-social communities into societies. It is, therefore, a life of political education.

However, the civilizing process is able to reflect liberal principles only to the extent that force actually can be removed from human relationships; at that point the identity between civility and politics is no longer sustainable. The boundaries of civility are formed by the continued existence of the non-social community and the unavoidability of the conditional use of force. This conditionality is not sufficient to accommodate civility because, as Collingwood understands it, treating someone civilly *means* abjuring force towards them.

The limits of civility here arise from the limits of politics; again, no civilization can completely abolish the elements of savagery and barbarism which it contains. As an ideal for assessing the dialectical achievement of a liberal political society complete civility is permanently out of reach. How, then, does civility relate to Collingwood's conception of politics as order? Consider Collingwood's example of queuing as a political good. Civility and politics correspond to the extent that both disavow disorder. They part company to the extent that politics is necessarily prone to disorder and necessarily involves the conditional use of force. If we construe civility as a second order ideal then it guides politics insofar as it encourages orderliness and discourages arbitrary, intimidatory or disrespectful treatment. Queuing as a practice is interesting from this point of view because it contains an element of collective self-restraint which links it to civility and yet lacks the element of authorized enforcement which is essential to politics. It mirrors self-government, but without the existence of rule.

The practice of queuing, as Collingwood describes it, is bound by specific rules; it is historically and culturally variable and it is not open necessarily to utilitarian explanation. Queuing, however, is not simply a matter of good manners; it reflects a political good, but of what kind? Rules of civility, unlike rules of etiquette, are moral requirements in terms of the seriousness of their prohibitions and the degree of blame which attaches to those who infringe them. They are closer to political virtues such as justice than they are to manners; further, if queuing is a political good it cannot be accounted for in terms of utility. Collingwood argues that 'it does not save time; it is definitely opposed to the interests of all the strongest and most active individuals; and it demands an extraordinary degree of discipline when you are at the end of the queue and the train is about to start' (*EPP*, p. 98). The good of queuing is a political good – 'orderliness, regularity, submission to a rule which applies equally to all persons' (*EPP*, p. 98); hence the resentment at the intrusion of disorder in the form of queue-jumping.

The problem here is that Collingwood's understanding of the political good as order per se comes too close to identifying it with the logic of civility. His description of queue-jumpers as objectionable because they *force themselves* without authority to the front of the queue makes this plain. But this results in the neglect of substantive moral considerations which cannot themselves be reclassified as constituents of order. In this respect, while Collingwood does not confuse the value of the practice of queuing with the purpose of any particular queue – for cheap beer, cup-final tickets or passports – he does seriously overlook the extent to which a principle of civility such as 'first come, first served' can satisfy the requirements of simplicity and order, but not address matters of justice in the form of merit, desert or need. Further, the practice of queuing may be disturbed for many different reasons, including bribery – one person paying another to queue for them, or paying another already in the queue to give up their place, or by a friend queuing for another, or by reserving a place. Our ways of addressing these contingencies do not derive from the notion of regularity as such, but draw on substantive considerations of tradition, character, disposition and circumstance. Additionally, Collingwood's claim that the rules of queuing apply equally to all is true only in the obvious minimal respect. People value their time unequally and this means that queuing as a practice necessarily involves orderliness with differential cost. Orderliness tells us little about whether those in the queue are present willingly or under some kind of duress – queue or starve. Queuing can discriminate against the weak who may be too ill to queue and it benefits those whose lives are flexible, allowing them to judge how much time is involved. Collingwood contrasts the English practice of queuing with the situation he found in France in which 'you had to fight all comers for your turn at the guichet' (*EPP*, p. 98); but what he fails to address is the adequacy of the concept of politics as order. As one instance of this, queuing satisfies the requirements of civility as a framework of action, but it can go no further. The weaknesses of queuing as a practice – its minimalism, discrimination, time costliness and procedural inflexibility – cannot be addressed through Collingwood's account of political rationality. Indeed, in this hierarchical structure politics as rule is prior to politics as utility, so any disadvantages inherent in an ordered practice can only be taken into account from within. Collingwood's concept of political action as order matches the imperatives of civility only by robbing politics of the claims of justice and neglecting collisions between such claims and the requirements of procedure.

Contemporary liberalism faces the problem of establishing a just political order while remaining neutral between different conceptions of the good. Collingwood rejects both utilitarianism and contractarianism as complete solutions and calls instead for a reconciliation of politics and civility based on the philosophy of mind and the theory of practical reason associated with it. It is noticeable, however, that for Collingwood civility as an ideal gains its most significant support from religion –

> The vital warmth at the heart of a civilization is what we call a religion. Religion is the passion which inspires a society to persevere in a certain way of life and to obey the rules which define it. (*EP*, p. 187)

This calling on religion to buttress the liberal practice of civility raises a number of predictable problems. First, Collingwood stresses religion as a source of internal strength; it is a 'personal relation', an 'inward flame', a 'vital warmth' (*SRC*, p. 15). The difficulty here is how religious belief understood as expressing an inner faith can square with civility understood as characterizing a shared practice; how can a private, emotional commitment give support to civility when the vocabulary of civility is public and intersubjective, formulated as a language involving rules and speech? Second, Collingwood's attempt to return liberalism to what he takes to be its Christian origins is consistent with his view of civility as an ideal embodying the principles of the Sermon on the Mount, but it raises doubts about the status of this ideal – is it an absolute presupposition of civility as practised in a particular culture? Is it a formal requirement of a just political order or a moral value which may on occasion conflict with other competing moral and political considerations? The social importance of civility as a political ideal derives from its setting limits on conduct, the recognition of which allows individuals the freedom to pursue their individual goals. Collingwood's explicit attempt to link Christianity, liberalism and civility leaves unclear the binding force of civility in predominantly secular or non-Christian societies.

This problem arises because Collingwood's account of the necessary incompleteness of civility as a first order ideal is extremely narrow and circumscribed by his understanding of society as a 'mix' of social and non-social elements. A political society is a conditional undertaking in which what Collingwood calls the dialectic of society and the dialectic of internal politics are necessarily incomplete. One mark of this is the need of each successive generation to find a political education; another is the permanent possibility of regression to the non-social condition in the form of criminality; and another is the unavoidability of force. But this is too restricted an account of the conditionality in politics which civility as an ideal has to face. In relation to political disagreements civility certainly has a strong bearing, in part, through the constraints it imposes on the agent. The disagreement must be genuine – a choice between one moral course and another rather than a merely prudentially desirable alternative. The agent must be able to treat such choices as real and not be predisposed to choose through fear or temptation. Civility requires these conditions because it imposes the constraint of self-respect. Collingwood, however, tends to overlook the depth of intransigence involved in some disagreements and dilemmas, so missing the sense in which moral choices are tested by a commitment to civility.

For liberals, lying is one thing, open to possible, conditional justification; cruelty, however, is quite another. What the liberal fears is not simply incivility manifested as servility, humiliation or exploitation, rule by those Collingwood terms 'gangsters' (*NL*, 40.35) or 'human brutes' (*NL*, 35.93), but barbarity, the deliberate attempt to put the process of civilization into reverse, to make society destitute of civility. Unlike savagery which is always relative, uncivilized to a degree and no more, barbarity is an active 'hostility towards civilization' (*NL*, 41.12). For Collingwood, however, the liberal fear here is unfounded for barbarism is at odds with itself – 'it is a *will to do nothing*, a will to acquiesce in the chaotic rule of emotion which it began by destroying. All it does is to assert itself as will and then deny itself as will' (*NL*, 36.94), and it must, therefore, fail – 'barbarists in the end have always been beaten' (*NL*, 45.94).

Collingwood understands civility as an appropriate response to the conditionality of politics, to the necessary imperfections of even a constitutional order. Living up to the ideal of civility means gradually reducing the incidence of servility, humiliation and exploitation, but how then do the civil speak to the uncivil? Rudeness and discourtesy may be pointed out, but can the exploitative be *persuaded* to relinquish their exploitation? If cruelty is a psychological state, can sadists be *argued out* of their compulsion? Barbarity, as Collingwood understands it, is outside the conceptual circle which enables conversation between the civil and the merely uncivil. It is outside the frame of rational discourse on which liberalism is conventionally thought to rely. But in what does this frame of rational discourse consist? By what kind of thinking is it known? Collingwood's answers to these questions are to be found essentially in his discussion of metaphysics and its relation to history. In his *Autobiography*, Collingwood, famously, describes his life's work as, in large part, bringing about 'a rapprochement between philosophy and history' (*A*, p. 77). In contemporary philosophy these questions resonate powerfully with the status of liberalism, and it is to these that we now turn.

Chapter 9
METAPHYSICS AND HISTORY

When Collingwood asserts that the central problem for modern philosophy to solve is the nature of its relation with history he is not just reporting on his own preoccupations. Of course, as a matter of biographical fact Collingwood reports faithfully, but the point of interest is not so much *that* this problem dominates his life's work, but *why* it did. What is it about history which explains why Collingwood places philosophy in such a close and not always amicable relationship with it? We find the answer in the elevated role Collingwood gives to history. Historical understanding is important not simply because it reflects the practice of historians. In Collingwood's view, historical understanding is more like a condition of human understanding in general than the preserve of one specific form of enquiry. History is a dimension of human existence. Human beings do not exist in a temporal vacuum, but in a complex historical present in which past and future are blended rather than sharply divided. In both thought and action human beings are creatures of history so, for Collingwood, 'history…is the life of the mind itself, which is not mind except so far as it both lives in historical process and knows itself as so living' (*IH*, p. 227).

Our historical nature, Collingwood may be read as saying, is a necessary feature of our humanity. We can no more stand outside history than we can reach beyond language. History and language constitute our humanity. But, then, if we are time-bound individuals able to visualize eternity only in our dreams how are we to evaluate our thoughts and actions? If there is no escape from history are we not benighted creatures who stumble aimlessly from one ungrounded project to the next? Collingwood's answer here is clear and resolute. Clarity is not shed on life – whether intellectual or practical – by seeking to transcend history. On the contrary, Collingwood construes our historicity as a source of strength. We do not observe the past from some godlike vantage point, nor is the past when understood on its own terms devoid of interest and stimulus to us. Most notably in his later writings, therefore, Collingwood attempts to bring metaphysics and philosophy into close and constructive relation with history and with liberalism. So, as Collingwood explains it, metaphysics is an historical science which reveals, among other sets of presuppositions, the basic structure of ideas of a liberal civilization, and which itself contributes to the civilizing process by exposing the errors of pseudo-metaphysics.

Of course, Collingwood's emphasis on history as a condition of life cannot leave philosophy untouched. If we exist as human beings at all we exist in history, but how, then, are we to reflect on this philosophically? Not, Collingwood insists, by thinking of philosophy as a method for discovering the essence of mind, human nature or human association. These concepts reflect human activities not as untensed states, but as processes subject to change and development. Does this disclaimer affect philosophy's autonomy in relation to history? Collingwood is easily misunderstood here. When he writes of problems in political philosophy – 'the history of political theory is not the history of different answers given to one and the same question, but the history of a problem more or less constantly changing, whose solution was changing with it' (*A*, p. 62) – it is not difficult to interpret him as saying that philosophical enquiries are fundamentally historical since the questions they raise do not exist in abstraction from place and time. This interpretation should be resisted, however. What Collingwood is emphasizing is the illusion involved in thinking that we can step outside the historical circumstances in which we think and act. Further, Collingwood's denial that there are permanent philosophical problems, independent of history, is a philosophical not an historical denial; one, indeed, that many philosophers not influenced by Collingwood find perfectly defensible.

Far from collapsing philosophy into its history Collingwood speaks about it by contrast with history as a second order activity which involves thinking about thought about the past. Collingwood writes:

> the philosopher has to think about the historian's mind, but in doing so he is not duplicating the work of the psychologist, for to him the historian's thought is not a complex of mental phenomena but a system of knowledge. He also thinks about the past, but not in such a way as to duplicate the work of the historian: for the past, to him, is not a series of events but a system of things known. One might put this by saying that the philosopher, in so far as he thinks about the subjective side of history, is an epistemologist, and so far as he thinks about the objective side a metaphysician; but that way of putting it would be dangerous as conveying a suggestion that the epistemological and metaphysical parts of his work can be treated separately, and this would be a mistake. (*IH*, p. 3)

At certain points in this passage Collingwood talks of philosophy as asking what makes history possible, engaging in a Kantian search for history's entitlement to knowledge. In considering philosophy in this way Collingwood is effectively reasserting its distinctive identity as second order thinking which is systematic, categorical and self-referential. In these characteristics philosophy finds its autonomy, but nothing in this gives philosophy a licence to reach beyond history. The idea that the philosophical standpoint lies outside any historical standpoint is a fantasy. Rather, Collingwood stresses the fruitful interrelationship between philosophical and historical thinking. He writes:

> history fertilized by philosophy is the history of the human spirit in its secular attempt to build itself a world of laws and institutions in which it can live as it wishes to live; and philosophy fertilized by history is the progressive raising and solving of the endless intellectual problems whose succession forms the inner side of this secular struggle. (*EPH*, p. 4)

When Collingwood wrote these words the philosopher he had in mind was, of course, Croce, but his description applies just as aptly to Hegel or, indeed, to Collingwood's own thought because it brings out very well the historically informed version of philosophical liberalism which he defended throughout his life. And, yet, is it not the case that the values which Collingwood's liberalism enshrines – civility, rational freedom, civilization – require a logically secure grounding if they are to be truly compelling? When Collingwood asserts that 'the moral ideal … cannot be conceived as a mere thought wholly divorced from existence' (*EPM*, p. 133) he is, in effect, forcing precisely this question on us. Is there a way of thinking, a form of argumentation, distinguishable within philosophy, which shows us how this can be achieved?

Collingwood's distinctive, radical and powerfully argued account of metaphysics is his attempt to answer this question. In 1933 Collingwood had defended the view that the ontological proof holds good in ethics as well as in logic, but in *An Essay on Metaphysics* ontology is explicitly abandoned. The traditional idea that metaphysics is a theory of pure being is rejected since a state of pure being must be a complete abstraction; hence, pure being cannot be a subject for metaphysical investigation. Nevertheless, Collingwood argues, ultimate states can be investigated if they are construed as absolute presuppositions. Such presuppositions take the form of those general claims about the nature of things which enable individuals to make sense of their world. They comprise the deep structure of a given society's beliefs; as such they are, in principle, unverifiable since to verify them would be to postulate the existence of something more ultimate. In other words, absolute presuppositions are not propositions, which means that the distinction between truth and falsity does not apply to them. They make up the logical bedrock of a society's world view. Beyond them there are only views from nowhere. In Collingwood's argument, the existence of absolute presuppositions gives metaphysics its determinate subject matter. He writes:

> Metaphysics is the attempt to find out what absolute presuppositions have been made by this or that person or group of persons, on this or that occasion or group of occasions, in the course of this or that piece of thinking. (*EM*, p. 47)

Further, since human societies exist in time, metaphysics as the science which uncovers their absolute presuppositions must be, as Collingwood puts it, an 'historical science' (*EM*, p. 66). The concern of metaphysics is not the nature of being, but the absolute presuppositions of a society at any given historical time. The task of metaphysics is, therefore, threefold. First, it must discover what any given society at a particular stage of its history believes about the world's general nature. Then it needs to identify its question and answer structure and to explain how questions and answers are related through the logic of presupposing, so distinguishing between relative presuppositions which stand relative to one question as its presupposition, to another as its answer, and absolute presuppositions which stand to all questions to which they are related only as presuppositions, never as answers. Finally, the task is to discover the process of conceptual change whereby one constellation of absolute presuppositions turns into another.

It should be readily apparent that Collingwood's reformulation of metaphysics is heavily dependent on his reprogramming of logic. In logic Collingwood describes himself as a revolutionary, but he understands his project in metaphysics as one of reform. How can we explain this difference? Collingwood's aim in logic is to *replace* propositional logic; in metaphysics, however, what he wishes to alter is not its traditional concern with the ultimate nature of things, but, rather, its traditional indifference to history. In other words, if metaphysics is to have a subject matter at all it must be consistent with the historical character of human thinking and acting. It is for this reason that Collingwood is a revolutionary in logic and a reformist in metaphysics.

It is tempting to regard Collingwood's demystification of metaphysics as little more than a sophisticated exercise in the history of ideas, but this is very far from the case. Metaphysics is not just a branch of intellectual history. As the study of past thought in the form of absolute presuppositions, metaphysics involves its own distinct methods and procedures. Collingwood describes it as an 'historical *science*' (*EM*, p. 66) (my emphasis), which suggests that logical analysis, in Collingwood's sense of question and answer, is as much a feature of its mode of enquiry as history. Indeed, it is not difficult to reconstruct metaphysical analysis on the Collingwoodian model. In terms of analysis, the metaphysician will be primarily concerned with disentangling the structure of a given question and answer complex, for example, the cosmological beliefs of the ancient Greeks or of the Renaissance (as Collingwood himself does in *The Idea of Nature*, Parts I and II). What such disentangling involves is the identification of the ways questions and answers work in any given complex and this means arranging them in their appropriate logical order. Further, the metaphysician will be concerned with what questions presuppose, either in the form of relative or absolute presuppositions. In establishing differences in kind here the metaphysician attends to what a world view takes for granted in order to remain what it is. Since relative presuppositions change through the standard process of questioning, and absolute presuppositions do not, charting the difference enables the metaphysician to reveal what an historical form of life rests on. In achieving this, metaphysics stands almost as close to history as genetics does to life since it is revelatory about what is fundamental in any picture of the world.

Metaphysics, in Collingwood's reformed version, is a science. It proceeds by logical analysis, but it is also an *historical* science which means that its methods must, in some sense, conform to the methods of history. As Collingwood forcibly makes the point:

> The problems of metaphysics are historical problems; its methods are historical methods…. We live in the twentieth century; there is no excuse for us if we do not know what the methods of history are. (*EM*, pp. 62–3)

On this basis, metaphysics will cease to be metaphysics if its methods are unhistorical. If, for example, the metaphysician thinks in terms of universal doctrines rather than absolute presuppositions then what is being practised is not metaphysics, but, in Collingwood's terms, 'pseudo-metaphysics' (*EM*, p. 47). Similarly, if the metaphysician asks which absolute presuppositions are true then the logic of absolute presuppositions has been misunderstood and this means again that what is being practised is not metaphysics, but pseudo-metaphysics.

Collingwood's attempt to square metaphysics with history is radical and it is not surprising, therefore, that among the thoughts that it has provoked are highly critical ones. Consider Collingwood's reformed metaphysics as an historical science. If metaphysics is, at least in part, historical, as Collingwood insists it must be, then its methods must be historical; which means that the metaphysician understands past thought by re-enacting it, in so far as the thought is reflective and its re-enactment permitted by the available evidence. But the metaphysician's subjects are absolute presuppositions which are, as we have discovered, thoughts of a special kind. Absolute presuppositions are not propositions. They are not open to verification, nor are they intended or chosen in any meaningful sense. The absolute presuppositions of a way of life are those it takes for granted. Thus, Collingwood writes:

> Metaphysics is concerned with absolute presuppositions. We do not acquire absolute presuppositions by arguing; on the contrary, unless we have them already arguing is impossible to us. Nor can we change them by arguing; unless they remained constant all our arguments would fall to pieces. We cannot confirm ourselves in them by 'proving' them; it is proof that depends on them, not they on proof. The only attitude towards them that can enable us to enjoy what they have to give us (and that means science and civilization, the life of rational animals) is an attitude of unquestioning acceptance. We must accept them and hold firmly to them; we must insist on presupposing them in all our thinking without asking why they should be thus accepted. (*EM*, p. 173)

Absolute presuppositions are not, therefore, matters of choice, reason-giving, argument or proof, but, then, if they are so far removed from cognitive awareness, how can the metaphysician re-enact them? The job of metaphysics is the detection of absolute presuppositions, but if it cannot detect them through re-enactment how can it proceed? One way forward here might be to interpret absolute presuppositions not as single units which are unre-enactable in themselves, but as features vital to *processes* of thinking. What the metaphysician wishes to explain, therefore, is the complete question and answer complex. By re-enacting the whole reflective process the metaphysician must eventually detect its absolute presuppositions, in other words, those presuppositions which are not answers to questions. The metaphysician proceeds, therefore, by reconstructing conceptual systems in much the same way as a chess master might detect the deep structure of a player's strategy by re-playing and, hence, following through, the moves in the game.

However, this way of rescuing Collingwood encounters a serious problem. If metaphysics is understood as systematic conceptual reconstruction then surely its historical character must drop out. For defenders of traditional metaphysics this will cause few difficulties, but Collingwood, clearly, cannot allow history to drop out. For Collingwood, what the metaphysician wishes to understand is not a timeless, intellectual problem, such as chess, but processes of thought involving standpoints often very different from his own. History is the essential element in Collingwood's reform of metaphysics and it is vital to his denial that there are 'eternal problems' (*A*, p. 67) in philosophy. Thus, Collingwood writes:

> ...metaphysics is no futile attempt at knowing what lies beyond the limits of experience, but is primarily at any given time an attempt to discover what the people of that time believe about the world's general nature...it is the attempt to discover the corresponding presuppositions of other peoples and other times, and to follow the historical process by which one set of presuppositions has turned into another. (*A*, p. 66)

Collingwood is quite explicit about his view of the connection between metaphysics and history:

> The question what presuppositions underlie the 'physics' or natural science of a certain people at a certain time is

as purely historical a question as what kind of clothes they wear. And this is the question that metaphysicians have to answer. (*A*, p. 66)

We have seen that if metaphysics in Collingwood's picture is to proceed at all then it cannot be by re-enactment. Metaphysics parts company from history because absolute presuppositions are not re-enactable, but do absolute presuppositions stand as Collingwood suggests to the metaphysics of their own time? In Collingwood's view, metaphysics makes explicit the absolute presuppositions which 'underlie' the thought of an age, but is this a persuasive account of metaphysical practice? Consider a work of metaphysics such as Plato's *Republic* from a Collingwoodian perspective. *The Republic*, in this interpretation, is not a utopia derived by reflection on the universal character of justice, but rather an examination of the presuppositions of one historically bounded way of life. And, yet, Plato's text contains much that is absent in any form from Athenian practice; indeed, it might be argued that it is because Plato's arguments comment on the world *sub specie aeternitatis* that any overlap between them and strictly fifth-century Greek preoccupations is marginal to their philosophical point. Similarly, how can Hegel's *Philosophy of Right*, to take a metaphysical text from the modern age, be understood as making explicit the presuppositions of early nineteenth-century Prussian politics when it develops ideas not contained in that practice? Are we to say that Hegel committed a metaphysical mistake by leaving out a presupposition, or by confusing an absolute for a relative one, or isn't it rather that Hegel speaks in a very different kind of voice?

Dissent from Collingwood here involves pointing out that metaphysicians do not just reflect what their world believes, nor do they just transform what their world believes by stating those beliefs as presuppositions. At least some metaphysical statements take the form not of presuppositions, but of propositions, which means that they can be attacked or defended in historical contexts different from their own. Hegel's *Science of Logic* professes to assert a series of atemporal truths. Aristotle's *Ethics* does not simply build on a bounded set of assumptions concerning nature, but urges on us a distinctive picture of the ethical life. To put this point succinctly, metaphysics is less contextually restricted than Collingwood asserts, since it is not only concerned with making explicit the presuppositions of its time, but with evaluating and criticizing them. Collingwood, of course, cannot permit metaphysics a critical role since to ask whether an absolute presupposition is true or false is to ask a question metaphysics is logically precluded from answering, but is this position sustainable? Is Collingwood able to practise what he preaches?

We must stress that in Collingwood's understanding metaphysics is allowed a little leeway for criticism. Metaphysicians can correct each other's views if it can be shown that a relative presupposition has been mistaken for an absolute one or if a presupposition has been detected with insufficient evidence to support it. Further, a metaphysics enlarged by history enables metaphysicians to grasp intellectual constellations different from their own and in so doing to compare them. This is not 'high class' (*EM*, p. 72) history, as Collingwood himself states, but it *is* part of metaphysics, and so we might query whether a comparison of absolute presuppositions could sensibly proceed without destroying their nature. Up to this point Collingwood has not allowed metaphysics to deviate too much in a critical direction, but he soon finds this difficult to sustain. We do not have to look far for the reason. Collingwood sees his reform of metaphysics as linked to the fate of European science and civilization. Indeed, he associates the logical positivist stance on ethics and politics with the rise of Fascism and, perhaps more significantly, with the weakness of liberalism in responding to it. So in a famous chapter in his *An Essay on Metaphysics* (*EM*, chap. 13, pp. 133–42) Collingwood asks his readers to consider how a civilization might decline from within. He suggests that we imagine a civilization whose members share a longstanding and predominant belief in truth established through systematic and ordered thinking. Truth so understood will have a significant presence in the religion of such a civilization as 'the gift of mental light' (*EM*, p. 133); in its philosophy as 'the method…of establishing standards by which on reflection truth can be distinguished from falsehood' (*EM*, p. 133); in its education as the induction of 'habits of orderly and systematic thinking' (*EM*, p. 134); and in its politics as 'predominantly the attempt to build up a common life by the methods of reason' (*EM*, p. 134). Now, suppose further, Collingwood suggests, that forces grow within this civilization which are deeply opposed to its fundamental presuppositions. Such forces Collingwood describes as 'an epidemic disease: a kind of epidemic withering of belief in the importance of truth' (*EM*, p. 136). A politics overtaken by them will find its belief in reasonableness supplanted by emotion, its belief in intelligent agreement displaced by the need for emotional solidarity and its belief in rational persuasion exchanged for conformity induced by terror. For Collingwood, these forces of irrationalism, as he calls them, proceed by stealth, disguising their real nature by taking on the appearance of the civilization they wish to destroy. Irrationalism is the parasite which aims to colonize its host. What Collingwood is describing here are the absolute presuppositions of a liberal culture buckling under threat, but how is metaphysics able to reinforce them if their logical efficacy is independent of their being true, dependent only on their being presupposed? Surely, Collingwood must now either concede that no one set of absolute presuppositions is more defensible than any other or attempt to *argue* for one as opposed to others. But we know that the absolute presuppositions of a way of life cannot be supported by arguing for them. So Collingwood states that a civilization threatened in this way can remain safe only so long as it retains its *belief* that its 'form of life' (*EM*, p. 140) is worth living. But, then, we want to ask, what is it that connects retaining the belief in the form of life with that form actually being worth living? At this point, Collingwood finds his metaphysical neutralism unsustainable and he defends one set of absolute presuppositions against others. Collingwood writes:

What has to be saved is not the way of living but the people who live in that way; and saving them means inducing them to live in a different way, a way that is not impracticable. The different way of living which these (Patristic) writers proposed for adoption was the way of living based upon the absolute presuppositions I have tried, in a partial and one-sided manner, to describe. The new way of living would involve a new science and a new civilization.

  The presuppositions that go to make up this 'Catholic Faith', preserved for many centuries by the religious institutions of Christendom, have as a matter of historical fact been the main or fundamental presuppositions of natural science ever since. They have never been its only absolute presuppositions; there have always been others, and these others have to some extent differed at different times. But from the fifth century down to the present day all these differences have played their changing parts against a background that has remained unchanged: the constellation of absolute presuppositions originally sketched by Aristotle, and described more accurately, seven or eight centuries later, by the Patristic writers under the name of the 'Catholic Faith'. (*EM*, pp. 226–7)

In defending the absolute presuppositions of the 'Catholic Faith' as forming the foundations of European science and liberalism Collingwood is, surely, asking metaphysics to do a great deal more than detect and criticize. In effect, he is requiring metaphysics to make a case for one body of presuppositions as opposed to others. He is claiming that one set of beliefs is better able to defend liberalism than any other. He is asserting, too, that a specifically Christian set of ideals gives us a better account of the worthwhile life than any other. But isn't this to think of the absolute presuppositions of the 'Catholic Faith' as matters of choice, of argument or of assertion; and isn't this what Collingwood says absolute presuppositions cannot be? Collingwood's position here seems to return metaphysics to its traditional indifference to history because he is forced to look to it for an ideal which guides the life not just of one society at any one historical time, but of human beings universally, as the 'Catholic Faith' purports to do. The nature of the link between thought and life is a major preoccupation in Collingwood's writings – it is to his view of the relation between philosophy and practice that we now direct our attention.

Chapter 10
PHILOSOPHY AND PRACTICE

In Collingwood's liberal politics the problem of civility lies in seeing how it can be extended both to its deliberate enemies *and* to those who simply do not share its assumptions. Contemporary philosophy, too, asks how liberal practices can be justified to those who are not liberals. Should an attempt be made to persuade non-liberals that they are required to be neutral between different conceptions of the good or should liberals try to show non-liberals that they are straightforwardly *wrong*? Further, are liberals better able to debate with non-liberals by abandoning any attempt to ground their beliefs in a set of ahistorical foundations, or is their liberalism logically dependent on precisely such a set? In his *Autobiography* Collingwood explores the dilemmas generated by these questions in a way that is characteristic of his own thinking *and* illustrative of the general difficulty. As Collingwood puts it, Mill's view that 'people ought to be allowed to think whatever they liked because it didn't really matter what they thought' (*A*, pp. 152–3), is false to the close relation between thought and practice and unstable from the standpoint of individual moral psychology. The failure of liberalism, for Collingwood, springs 'not from weakness or falsity in the principles of liberalism itself, but from the failure…to put these principles consistently into practice' (*EPP*, p. 186).

Collingwood's ideal of civil virtue is not simply a particular conception of the good that he happens to share with others. Civility is not just a preference. Collingwood understands it to be a formal value which, in any particular political society, coexists in various ways with the different types and sources of incivility. Civility as a formal criterion of conduct belongs at the heart of the liberal creed since it requires

> the dialectical solution of all political problems: that is, their solution through the statement of opposing views and their free discussion until, beneath this opposition, their supporters have discovered some common ground on which to act. (*EPP*, p. 177)

This 'common ground' does not consist of preference construed as a neutral standard of assessment, but neither is it an objective standpoint external to the practice in question. Collingwood insists that an individual 'cannot criticize the civilization of his society from a detached, external point of view' (*NL*, p. 499), but what, then, is philosophy's role here? How is it possible for philosophy to speak to life?

In his answers to these questions Collingwood repeatedly stresses that philosophy cannot stand remote from life. From *Speculum Mentis* to *An Essay on Metaphysics* the practical value of philosophy is a constant theme. In 1924 philosophy is given the task of overcoming error by restoring the unity of thought and action. In 1940 Collingwood through philosophy warns European civilization of the dangers which face it. The refusal of analytical philosophy to address life in large measure explains Collingwood's aloofness from it. For him, no sharp distinction exists between analytical and speculative thought. The claim of analytical philosophy to be propaedeutic, a methodology uniquely suited to clarifying the workings of language, devoid of any strong implications for life, is false. By disclaiming possession of any theories about its nature, analytical philosophy is, in fact, attempting to insulate itself from criticism. Where Collingwood succeeds powerfully is in forcing these unspoken assump-tions to the surface and, in so doing, revealing them for what they are – not technical, ahistorical propositions, neutral in regard to practice, but a context-bound set of ideas which, like any other when made explicit, is open to critical assessment and supersession.

For Collingwood, there is one area of life about which the analytical philosopher cannot be neutral. In denying that moral conduct is affected by their account of it, realists actually 'give a false account to themselves of their own experience, so deform that experience that it loses its highest qualities and actually becomes something not altogether unlike what they falsely think it' (*SM*, p. 295). In other words, realists who assert that values do not operate like facts must either complacently exclude their own moral beliefs or accept that they are wrong about what keeps them morally alert. It is no accident that in his *Autobiography* Collingwood borrows Berkeley's phrase 'minute philosophers' to head the chapter (chap. 3) where he attacks modern defenders of such doctrines. Indeed, Berkeley's description of the effects of minute philosophy brings out very well what Collingwood wants to say about realism:

> We are a very merry nation indeed: young men laugh at the old; children despise their parents; and subjects make a jest of the government; happy effects of the minute philosophy! (*AL*, p. 107)

A disordered polity, Berkeley may be read as saying, reflects disordered thought, and Collingwood would have agreed with him. From the mid-1930s, however, what Collingwood saw was not simply a civilization in chaos, but one engaged in mass self-destruction. In the aftermath of the failure of Republicanism in the Spanish Civil War and with German territorial ambitions becoming ever more threatening Collingwood wrote a short piece called 'Man Goes Mad' (*EPP*, pp. 177–86, extracted); Collingwood's title interestingly anticipates H. G. Well's 1945 essay 'Mind at the End of Its Tether'. In 'Man Goes Mad' Collingwood states that 'the plainest political fact of our time is the widespread collapse of…liberalism' (*EPP*, p. 177) and he calls for a liberalism which puts its 'principles consistently into practice' (*EPP*, p. 186). There is no doubt that after 1936 Collingwood's writing becomes increasingly preoccupied with politics, more specifically with how an intellectual response can be formulated which sustains liberals in times of crisis. However, such a response involves a great deal more than delivering liberals from their sense of private despair. Collingwood concludes his *Autobiography*, published in 1939, with a statement of intent which is as much political as personal – 'I know that all my life I have been engaged unawares in a political struggle, fighting against those things in the dark. Henceforth I shall fight in the daylight' (*A*, p. 167).

What Collingwood determines to fight against is irrationalism. How it is to be fought is through philosophy; if the disordered world reflects disordered thought then, Collingwood reasons, we should attend to the world by revealing and destroying the errors which have corrupted it. Further, if the battle is one of ideas it has to be joined in the daylight – philosophy can confront its intellectual opponents in no other way. But this move (which follows, incidentally, the great tradition of liberal enlightenment thinking on the question of what philosophy can say about life) assumes that philosophy can actually generate ideals by which to live. Philosophy's residence, this move implies, is not distant from the world, but in the closest proximity to it. The gap between theory and practice can be closed. Thus, as Wittgenstein asks:

What is the use of studying philosophy at all if all that it does is enable you to talk with some plausibility about some abstruse questions of logic, etc., and if it does not improve your thinking about the important questions of everyday life, if it does not make you more conscientious than any journalist in the use of the *dangerous* phrases such people use for their own ends. (*LWAM*, p. 39)

The nature of the connection between philosophy and life is not, however, just a matter of putting certain ideas into practice; it is also a philosophical problem.

Moral philosophers are here in a unique position since they are inextricably bound up in the practices they wish to examine and, possibly, defend. Individuals may choose to become scientists, but all are moral agents; all are members of political communities. Moral philosophers are, therefore, not only observers, but necessarily participants in the very activities they wish to investigate. Thus, conclusions about the nature of ethical life will depend, in part, on purely philosophical considerations, but they will also depend on the kind of practical insight the philosopher brings to the activity being examined. Further, the point of the philosophical exercise is not limited to deepening the understanding, for philosophical conclusions may have to be defended in the practical world when they are threatened.

Similarly, philosophical difficulties in ethics arise out of the practical world, and the ways such difficulties are addressed by philosophy can involve implications for practice. But the acknowledgement that ethics can have implications for life falls a long way short of Collingwood's ambition for it. In other words, by giving philosophy the strategic role in the battle to defend liberalism Collingwood would seem to be placing it in the closest possible relation to life, but what would that relation be? Clearly, Collingwood's position is remote from Oakeshott's view that attempts by philosophy to influence conduct merely end as 'holiday excursions' (*EM*, p. 1) from its proper subject of concern, but it is worth stressing that Collingwood does not start from the opposite extreme. He accepts that philosophy

cannot descend like a *deus ex machina* upon the stage of practical life and, out of its superior insight into the nature of things, dictate the correct solution for this or that problem in morals, economic organization, or international politics. (*EPP*, p. 166)

In issuing this disclaimer Collingwood is surely right. The idea that philosophy is in the business of providing 'correct solutions' to practical problems suggests that without the enlightenment moral theory can provide, moral agents blunder about in the dark, making judgements which are from the standpoint of theory semi-literate. In this picture, the decisions made by agents and governments are open to correction by theory in much the same way as poor grammar or spelling is corrected by etymology. Such a picture is, of course, mistaken because it is true neither to theory nor to life, and Collingwood is surely right to reject it. He writes:

But people do not need, and would not tolerate, such guidance from moral theorists. To decide how he ought to behave is the task of the agent himself; a task in which the moral theorist can help, if he can, only because he too is a moral agent, and the moral agent in his degree already a moral theorist. (*EPM*, p. 131)

How, then, can philosophy speak to life? Collingwood's answers reflect his admiration for T. H. Green. First, by confronting scepticism philosophy shows that human beings have rights and duties which are not reducible to matters of interest and expediency. Second, philosophy generates ideals by which to live; in so doing it identifies the lack of clarity which often makes moral disagreement more intransigent than it need be; it establishes that political problems are not insoluble *in principle*, and it provides a standard against which human beings can assess their various individual and institutional attempts to act virtuously towards each other. Indeed, Collingwood sometimes writes as if the philosopher is emblematic in this respect:

...the moral philosopher in describing virtue must himself, in his work as a thinker, display some at least of the virtues he describes – sincerity, truthfulness, perseverance, courage, and justice.... (*EPM*, pp. 132–3)

Third, in construing human activities as expressive of reasons as opposed to mere preferences philosophy formulates a theory of practical reason, the main forms of which – utility, right and duty – are arranged hierarchically, each representing a more comprehensive and, hence, more fully realized stage in the development of human consciousness.

Nothing in this manifesto requires philosophy to provide detailed guidance for conduct. General rules have to be applied, and abandoned or expressed differently when they encounter cases not covered in the rule's original formulation. In these circumstances, Collingwood argues, philosophy is displaced by history. He writes:

We study history in order to see more clearly into the situation in which we are called upon to act. Hence the plane on which, ultimately, all problems arise is the plane of 'real' life: that to which they are referred for their solution is history. (*A*, p. 114)

Collingwood insists, of course, that no historian can, qua historian, prophesy the future, but human societies express their members' hopes and fears for future generations as well as their traditional ways of behaving. In times of great political strain, when confidence in the future is threatened, the value of history is limited since it concerns 'only one aspect of the present – how it came to be what it is' (*EPH*, p. 139), and it must, therefore, abdicate in favour of philosophy. But what can philosophy say here? Can Collingwood's manifesto be delivered?

What Collingwood believed himself to be witnessing in the years after 1938 was a civilization destroying itself from within. Liberalism in its historic confrontation with barbarism had criminally failed to live up to its ideals. But, in Collingwood's own terms, how else could liberalism assert the worth of its ideals except by deploying the presuppositions peculiar to them? To say that liberalism's failure is one of nerve rather than principle is to say nothing more than when confidence returns its principles will be as secure as ever, but this is precisely the issue at stake. Collingwood does not cast civility as an ideal to history to be devoured by the relativist sharks, but in his later thought the tension between civility as an ideal governing political life and civility as embodied in a specific political discourse reflects deep strains between philosophy and history which he never completely eliminates. We can bring out this difficulty in another way. Collingwood argues that the decline of liberalism is due, in large measure, to its indifference to the separation of moral theory from moral practice. The culprit is, of course, realism. Here is Collingwood's version of a realist lecture in moral philosophy:

> Remember the great principle of realism, that nothing is affected by being known. That is as true of human action as of anything else. Moral philosophy is only the theory of moral action: it can't therefore make any difference to the practice of moral action. People can act just as morally without it as with it. I stand here as a moral philosopher; I will try to tell you what acting morally is, but don't expect me to tell you how to do it. (*A*, p. 48)

Notice, however, that the disavowal with which this passage concludes is as much a feature of liberalism as it is of realism. Collingwood clearly considers that liberalism contains values such as civility and rational freedom which are worth defending, but these are largely negative ideals. They specify freedom of choice – in Collingwood's words, 'to decide how he ought to behave is the task of the agent himself' (*EPM*, p. 131) – but not the choice itself. Moral agents are, in Collingwood's picture, as much as in that of the traditional liberal, sole guardians of the moral will. But in terms of individual moral psychology what, in Collingwood's view, roots an agent's choices? What do liberals fall back on when their beliefs are challenged?

From the point of view of the capacity of philosophy to influence life Collingwood's answer here seems noticeably insecure. Behind the flux of each individual's everyday behaviour it is possible, Collingwood believes, to detect a core of deeply held principles which are systematic, harmonious and vital to any particular individual's life. They constitute, as it were, the absolute moral presuppositions of that life. Individuals often do not need, and are sometimes reluctant or unable, to state them explicitly, either to themselves or openly to others. If they are questioned about them individuals can be surprised and puzzled. But Collingwood is in no doubt that such presuppositions exist and that they are essential. They determine who we are and what we do. They may crack under pressure if the strain of supporting them is too great. When asked about them, Collingwood writes, 'people are apt to be ticklish' (*EM*, p. 31), so a scientist asked about his belief that every event has a cause might reply –

> That is a thing we take for granted in my job. We don't question it. We don't try to verify it. It isn't a thing anybody has discussed, like microbes or the circulation of the blood. It is a thing we just take for granted. (*EM*, p. 31)

But how, on the basis of this account of moral psychology, can philosophy influence life? Certainly, the liberal's belief in freedom is not like that of the scientist's belief in microbes or the circulation of the blood in being verifiable, or discoverable in any straightforward sense, but neither is it just taken for granted. Rather than operating as an unquestionable presupposition of liberalism, a belief in freedom is open to scrutiny both in terms of its nature and its extent.

So, if Collingwood wants a philosophy able to speak to liberals, he must, surely, drop his picture of moral psychology. We may grant Collingwood that, for liberals, reflecting on their deepest beliefs involves examining their prejudices but, then, isn't this another way of saying that liberals cannot take their beliefs for granted?

Of course, many of the difficulties that Collingwood faces in his attempt to bring philosophy to bear on life are common to all such attempts. Thus, utilitarianism, for example, in seeking to talk to life on its terms only, invariably finds that in life moral vocabularies are both more numerous and more diverse than it can admit. Similarly, Collingwood in addressing life through the moral language generated by his theory of practical reason is confronted by a wide range of moral voices which do not share the theory's assumptions. The transcendence of Collingwood's ethics is no guarantee of its being all-inclusive of life. Further, it is not unusual to find examples of philosophers who write about politics from a similar moral position, but whose strictly philosophical views are poles apart. Collingwood differs from Russell, for example, in terms of his conception of philosophy, his understanding of its method and what it can show to be true, but in relation to politics their affinities are striking. Both share the belief in a civilization grounded in reason, the vital significance of education and the need to call an errant world to order. Both, notably, have reputations as moral mavericks, laying the moral law down to others, but not always with a full appreciation of the problems others face. Such difficulties are, however, standard in the attempts made by philosophers to bring philosophy closer to life. In different ways they present a challenge to Collingwood's belief in the essential unity of thought and action because they involve disjunctions. They raise interesting disaffinities between intellect and life.

CONCLUSION

Famously, Collingwood advises philosophers against writing about his work (*A*, pp. 118–19), suggesting that they should instead get on with their own thinking about the subject. Equally famously, many philosophers find that they can make no progress in their work without taking Collingwood into account. Collingwood did not, however, understand his own relation with other philosophers in quite these terms. If he had, then Vico might have remained unread and the pages of Croce's *Estetica* might have been left unturned. These are, of course, only possibilities, but what we can confidently assert is that once philosophical arguments are on the page it matters not one jot that they belonged originally to Plato, to Hegel, say, or to Wittgenstein. They are now in the public domain and will be treated as such. Indeed, this is precisely what Collingwood teaches – that since past and present overlap, no sharp distinction exists between considering philosophers historically and placing them within a contemporary debate. All thought is, to some degree, critically re-enacted thought, so in thinking about Collingwood's arguments we are retracing his steps, sometimes agreeing with his conclusions, at others feeling that more should have been said; sometimes noticing that a process of thought is incomplete, at others that Collingwood's difficulty in taking his argument forward is also ours.

In this book we have made Collingwood's thinking part of our own and we have listened to his voice as intently as we would to that of a contemporary. Readers will recall that in my Introduction I spoke of having a conversation with Collingwood. Differences of opinion have been aired and disagreements expressed. We no more share a common estimate of Collingwood and what he says in philosophy than he and his contemporaries did of Croce or Hegel.

In this short introduction I have concentrated on Collingwood's main arguments and my reaction to them. This is not the place to attempt a survey of Collingwood's philosophical achievements since these largely depend on how much stimulation philosophers gain from his ideas. Indeed, in judging Collingwood many philosophers have been content to be selective, picking out what they take to be the most provocative and fruitful arguments (say, on the nature of language) rather than attempting to digest his work wholesale. Neither is this the place for last words on Collingwood, for last words, except in one obviously limiting case, have a notorious habit of failing to live up to their name. Collingwood is often marked out in twentieth-century philosophy as a lonely and isolated intellect. There is some justification for this. Collingwood did not philos-ophize in the manner of those within the analytic tradition and, yet, in aesthetics and in the philosophy of history his insights shape our own. In political philosophy Collingwood's attempt to create an historically informed version of philosophical liberalism anticipates and, to some degree, shares many of liberal theory's later frailties and hesitancies. Collingwood, as we have seen, could never tolerate a too rigorous separation of philosophy from life, and if, at times, philosophy in his hands seems to be practised too close to the sound of battle then our own thought on the subject is more invigorated as a result.

Collingwood wished to speak for a civilization he thought was in decline from within as much as under attack from without, but the voices in which he chose to express that support are very different. One speaks of the human spirit in movement, the other attempts to penetrate to the unchanging essence of things. The first of these is history, the second, of course, is philosophy. Collingwood's sustained preoccupation with the complex relations between these forms of thought reflects what I have termed his 'big worry', namely, the nature of the unity of thought and action. Sometimes Collingwood speaks clearly to us as an historian, at others as a philosopher; on some occasions he writes as a liberal, on others as a Christian. Collingwood wished it possible for a single person to be all these things, but often *we* read him as saying that in all consistency it is not. Does the problem belong to us or to Collingwood?

The question whether a man's views are true or false does not arise until we have found out what they are. Hence the reader's thought must always move from comprehension to criticism…. Criticism…may be regarded as a single operation: the bringing to completeness of a theory which its author has left incomplete…in practice, it is well known that a man's best critics are his pupils, and his best pupils the most critical. (*EPM*, pp. 217–20)

BIBLIOGRAPHY OF WORKS BY OTHERS

Ayer, A. J., *Philosophy in the Twentieth Century* (Weidenfeld and Nicolson, London, 1982)

Berkeley, G., *Works*, edited by A. A. Luce and T. E. Jessop, vol. 3, *Alciphron or the Minute Philosopher* (Thomas Nelson, London, 1950)

Carrington, C., *Rudyard Kipling, His Life and Work*, revised edition (Macmillan, London, 1978)

Malcolm, N., *Ludwig Wittgenstein: A Memoir* (Oxford University Press, Oxford, 1962)

Oakeshott, M., *Experience and its Modes* (Cambridge University Press, Cambridge, 1933)

Russell, B., *Fact and Fiction* (George Allen and Unwin, London, 1961)

Ryle, G., *Collected Papers*, vol. 1 (Hutchinson, London, 1971)

Wittgenstein, L., *On Certainty*, edited by G. E. M. Anscombe and G. H. von Wright, translated by Denis Paul and G. E. M. Anscombe (Blackwell, Oxford, 1969)

Wittgenstein, L., *Philosophical Investigations*, translated by G. E. M. Anscombe (Blackwell, Oxford, 1953)

Wittgenstein, L., *Tractatus Logico-Philosophicus*, translated by D. F. Pears and B. F. McGuinness (Routledge and Kegan Paul, London, 1961)

GUIDE TO FURTHER READING

WORKS BY COLLINGWOOD

a) Philosophical Books

Religion and Philosophy (Macmillan, London, 1916)

Speculum Mentis (Clarendon Press, Oxford, 1924)

Outlines of a Philosophy of Art (Oxford University Press, London, 1925)

An Essay on Philosophical Method (Clarendon Press, Oxford, 1933)

The Principles of Art (Clarendon Press, Oxford, 1938)

An Autobiography (Oxford University Press, London, 1939); reprinted with a new introduction by Stephen Toulmin (Clarendon Press, Oxford, 1978)

An Essay on Metaphysics (Clarendon Press, Oxford, 1940)

The First Mate's Log (Oxford University Press, London, 1940); reprinted with an introduction by Peter Johnson (Thoemmes Press, Bristol, 1994)

The New Leviathan (Clarendon Press, Oxford, 1942); (revised edition, with additional material, edited by David Boucher (Clarendon Press, Oxford, 1992)

The Idea of Nature, edited by T. M. Knox (Clarendon Press, Oxford, 1945)

The Idea of History, edited by T. M. Knox (Clarendon Press, Oxford, 1946); revised edition, edited by Jan van der Dussen (Clarendon Press, Oxford, 1993)

b) Translations in Philosophy

Croce, B., *An Autobiography*, with a Preface by J. A. Smith (Clarendon Press, Oxford, 1927)

Croce, B., *The Philosophy of Giambattista Vico* (H. Latimer, London, 1913)

Guido de Ruggiero, *Modern Philosophy* (George Allen and Unwin, London, 1921) with A. H. Hannay

Guido de Ruggiero, *The History of European Liberalism* (Oxford University Press, London, 1927)

c) Collections in Philosophy

Essays in the Philosophy of Art, edited by A. Donagan (Indiana University Press, Bloomington, 1964)

Essays in the Philosophy of History, edited by W. Debbins (University of Texas Press, Austin, Texas, 1965)

Essays in Political Philosophy, edited by David Boucher (Clarendon Press, Oxford, 1989)

Faith and Reason, Essays in the Philosophy of Religion, edited by L. Rubinoff (Quadrangle, Chicago, 1968)

d) Correspondence

Johnson, Peter, *The Correspondence of R. G. Collingwood. An Illustrated Guide* (The Collingwood Society, 1998)

WORKS BY OTHERS

a) Bibliographies

Burchnall, Ruth A., *Catalogue of the Papers of Robin George Collingwood* (1889–1943) (Dep Collingwood 1–28; Bodleian Library, Oxford, 1994)

Dreisbach, Christopher, *R. G. Collingwood: A Bibliographic Checklist* (Philosophy Documentation Centre, Bowling Green, Ohio, 1993)

Taylor, Donald S., *R. G. Collingwood: A Bibliography* (Garland Publishing Inc., New York and London, 1988)

b) Secondary Literature (Books)

Boucher, D., *The Social and Political Thought of R. G. Collingwood* (Cambridge University Press, Cambridge, 1989)

Donagan, A., *The Later Philosophy of R. G. Collingwood* (Clarendon Press, Oxford, 1962); 2nd edition, revised (University of Chicago Press, Chicago, 1985)

Dray, W. H., *History as Re-enactment, R. G. Collingwood's Idea of History* (Clarendon Press, Oxford, 1995)

Hinz, M., *Self-Creation and History, Collingwood and Nietzsche on Conceptual Change* (University Press of America, Lanham, Maryland, 1994)

Hogan, J. P., *Collingwood and Theological Hermeneutics* (University Press of America, Lanham, 1989)

Johnston, W. M., *The Formative Years of R. G. Collingwood* (Martinus Nijhoff, The Hague, 1967)

Kanichai, C., *R. G. Collingwood's Philosophy of History* (Pontifical Institute of Theology and Philosophy, Alwaye, India, 1981)

Mink, L. O., *Mind, History and Dialectic, The Philosophy of R. G. Collingwood* (Indiana University Press, Bloomington, 1969)

Olivetti, A. G., *Due Saggi Sue R. G Collingwood* (Liviana Editrice, Padua, Veneto, 1977)

Rubinoff, L., *Collingwood and the Reform of Metaphysics, A Study in the Philosophy of Mind* (University of Toronto Press, Toronto, 1970)

Russell, A. F., *Logic, Philosophy and History* (University Press of America, Lanham, 1984)

Saari, H., *Re-Enactment: A Study in R. G. Collingwood's Philosophy of History* (Abo Akademi, Turku, Sweden, 1984)

Skagestad, P., *Making Sense of History* (Universitetsforlaget, Oslo, 1975)

Van der Dussen, W. J., *History as a Science, The*

Philosophy of R. G. Collingwood (Martinus Nijhoff, The Hague, 1981)

c) Secondary Literature (Collections)

Boucher, D., Connelly, J. and Modood, T. (editors), *Philosophy, History and Civilization, Interdisciplinary Perspectives on R. G. Collingwood* (University of Wales Press, Cardiff, 1995)

Krausz, M., *Critical Essays on the Philosophy of R.G. Collingwood* (Clarendon Press, Oxford, 1972)

d) Collingwood Society Publications

Collingwood Studies, vol. 1, 1994, *Life and Thought*, edited by David Boucher

Collingwood Studies, vol. 2, 1995, *Perspectives*, edited by David Boucher and Bruce Haddock

Collingwood Studies, vol. 3, 1996, *Letters from Iceland and other Essays*, edited by David Boucher and Bruce Haddock

Collingwood Studies, vol. 4, 1997, *Variations: Themes from the Manuscripts*, edited by David Boucher and Bruce Haddock